Simon Dawson lives off-grid on a self-sufficient smallholding on Exmoor with his wife, two Great Danes and 187 assorted farm animals. He is the author of three books – *The Self Sufficiency Bible*, *Pigs in Clover* and *The Sty's the Limit* – and has contributed literally hundreds of articles to newspapers and magazines.

When not out on the farm or writing, he teaches how to be self-sufficient in today's busy world, with courses and workshops on butchery, curing, bread and butter making and animal husbandry. He is also an after-dinner speaker and radio presenter.

OTHER TITLES

Making Your Own Cheese
How To Make Your Own Sausages
Fermenting Food for Healthy Eating
How To Make Your Own Cordials and Syrups
How To Make Perfect Panini
Everyday Bread from Your Bread Machine

Make Your Own Butter:

Delicious recipes and flavourings for homemade butter

Simon Dawson

....

A HOW TO BOOK

ROBINSON

ROBINSON

First published in Great Britain in
2019 by Robinson

10 9 8 7 6 5 4 3 2 1

Text copyright © Simon Dawson,
2019
Illustrations copyright © David
Andrassy

A CIP catalogue record for this book
is available from the British Library.

ISBN: 978-1-47214-228-3

Typeset by Basement Press, Glaisdale
Printed and bound in Great Britain by
CPI Group (UK) Ltd, Croydon CR0 4YY

Papers used by Robinson are
from well-managed forests and
other responsible sources.

MIX
Paper from
responsible sources
FSC® C104740

Robinson
An imprint of
Little, Brown Book Group
Carmelite House
50 Victoria Embankment
London EC4Y 0DZ

An Hachette UK Company
www.hachette.co.uk

www.littlebrown.co.uk

How To Books are published by
Robinson, an imprint of Little,
Brown Book Group. We welcome
proposals from authors who have
first-hand experience of their
subjects. Please set out the aims
of your book, its target market and
its suggested contents in an email
to howtobooks@littlebrown.co.uk

Contents

INTRODUCTION

Welcome to the amazing world of butter. Actually, I feel an introduction should be made, because if you've only ever bought butter from the shops, then you've not really met. Not properly.

It's a bit like homemade bacon, or homemade ketchup: the first time you come across homemade butter there's a very definite 'Wow!' moment. But let's be honest, no matter how amazing it is, your next thought is likely to be, 'It must be incredibly complicated to make. Time consuming. Messy. Fiddly. Totally impractical,' because the human brain loves a bit of negativity.

Well, what if I told you it was none of those. In fact you can banish those negative thoughts right here, right now. Making your own butter at home is simple, clean and perfectly practical. More than that it's fun.

Can kids get involved? Yes! Grandkids? Of course. Teenagers? If you can get them out of bed or off the computer. Busy mums, football dads, cruisers, crooners and lounge lizards. Yes, yes, yes, yes. This is something open to anyone and everyone.

So that's the who covered, now for the why. Why make your own butter at home?

Because of the flavour. Because you are in control. Because you know exactly what's in it. Because it satisfies that urge to be creative. Because it's different. Because it's impressive. Because women and children have been churning butter for thousands of years and it would be heartbreaking if the skill died out. Because it is a skill, and one that once learned will stand you in good stead for the rest of your life. Because your dinner party/restaurant/ date -night meal will rise to the next level. Because it's a conversation grabber. Because it's bragging rights. Because it's comforting. But most of all, because what you eat, and what you share with your family and friends is important, and if it's homemade, with love, then that will come shining through.

Oh, and it's really easy to do.

Now, if you consider that butter has been around for about 10,000 years, and when you factor in man and woman's desire for creativity and experiment, it gives us a lot of buttery goodness to talk about. So cramming all that collected knowledge on butter into a single book is going to be tight. In order to have it make any sense, I've divided the book into four chapters:

- What you need to know about butter
- Making butter
- Getting creative
- Recipes with butter as the headline act

Each section will introduce you to that aspect of butter and tell you what the aims are, and how we can achieve them with minimal equipment, ingredients, tears and tantrums. We'll then chat through the how-to guides in such a way that it's fun and entertaining as well as practical and inspiring. By the time we finish you'll know everything there is to know about butter, plus we'll have some laughs along the way.

But all of that counts for nothing if you don't end up with your own homemade butter. It's my job to get you so enthralled that you'll literally stop at nothing to break out the food mixer and start churning – and you will, I promise you, you will.

For years now I have run courses on every aspect of smallholding and self-sufficiency for people across the world, and it's always the same. My wife Debbie and I fill two days with everything from discussing the sex life of chickens (hilarious, don't get me started) to curing bacon, and at the end people stand there and confidently state, 'I've loved everything, but the one thing I'll definitely take away is to make butter!'

Just because this is a book the goal is no different.

CHAPTER 1

What you need to know about butter

In this section we'll discuss what you need to know. It's the background. The origins story. It's like *Batman Begins*, but for butter. We'll find out what butter is, where it comes from, what's in it, and enough detail to satisfy the biggest butter geeks.

What we'll discover is that butter is a whole world unto itself. The fact that we take a little and spread it over our toast is the tip of the butter mountain. There's so much more to it!

This part of the book is about equipping you with information, because the more you understand about what we're doing and why, the more likely you are to find the butter-making experience enjoyable, and easy.

For instance, butter making is the art of churning double cream (milk with a high percentage of fat). Now, if you happen to have a cow or a goat in your back garden that you can wander out and milk, so much the better. Otherwise, I'm betting you need to pop down to the shops for your ingredients. But with so many varieties of cream available, which one should you choose? Which one will give you the best tasting butter? The best yield? We'll answer all of these questions and many more.

For this part of the book, you won't need any equipment or ingredients, other than maybe a cup of tea and a packet of biscuits, which are entirely optional.

A SHORT HISTORY OF BUTTER

Truth is, nobody really knows when and where butter making began, but chances are it's going to be around the time man first domesticated cattle in about 8500 BC.

Aurochs, or ancient ox, are the predecessors to today's cattle, although if you saw aurochs and modern cows mixing in a field you'd struggle to believe they were the same family. Aurochs were far bigger, coarser and yet to have manners bred into them. Put it this way, you wouldn't walk your dog through a field of them.

Around the time Stone Age man began wondering if flint wasn't a bit overrated, and perhaps there was something to this gardening malarkey after all, the 'all new' Neolithic era began to take shape. Down-with-the-kids Neolithic man took a monumental decision. He decided to capture and pen up a small number of aurochs, which in itself was no mean feat. Although common throughout the Near East, the prospect of actually capturing a few of these beasts must have been fraught with terror and danger. But somehow they pulled it off. This small number, we believe to be about 80, are the forefathers of all of today's cattle. It must have taken several generations to calm the wild beasts, and a few more before they could milk them, but you imagine them getting there at some point. And thus the dairy industry was born.

But if those brave Neoliths were the first to make butter, it was the Greeks that named it. *Bouturon*, Greek for 'cow cheese', became the preferred term, replacing, 'Oh, you know, that yellow, slippery, shiny stuff.' However, it wasn't until 2500 BC that the first written account made mention of it. Carved on a stone tablet, it's doubtful it was a shopping list, chiselled neatly below 'bread, peas and something to wipe my bum with', and history is all the poorer for that.

Around this same time, 2500 BC, some industrious Brits were busy with a little construction we like to call Stonehenge. Of course now we know Stonehenge as an amazing sight that sends shivers down your spine when you look at it, but back then, according to English Heritage, it was a building site with party benefits and, surprisingly, one of the first mentions of butter in the UK. It seems ancient Brits grafted by day and tore it up at night, drinking and partying and eating bread smothered in heaps of butter with meat; and thus, one of the wonders of the world was built – the open sandwich. And Stonehenge.

However, it is fair to say that early man struggled over quite what to do with butter. At one point it was used as a barrier against the cold by smearing it on their naked bodies, with men around the globe proclaiming, 'Ooh pet, it's a bit parky out, hand me the butter dish. Are you not feeling a bit chilly yourself?'

Then for a while it was a fuel for early lamps, although that didn't catch on either, which is no surprise to anyone who has tried lighting a fire in the wilderness by striking a match onto a tub of Utterly Butterly.

Such was the mystique that surrounded butter in these early days, it was decided the gods would be delighted if it was used in religious ceremonies as they were all over anything new. Presumably the gods lapped it up, although not literally, and continue to do so as it's still used in some religions.

As we dot down through the centuries towards the modern era, it seems people found many different uses for butter. For example, the Egyptians used it as an eye ointment. The Romans favoured it as a skin cream, and the Greeks used it to slick back their hair, though it was probably best to avoid being caught out in the midday sun for fear of melting.

It's been used in drinks, as medication and for fertility (probably deriving from the times when they were rubbing it over their naked bodies to 'keep warm'). And in Britain we spread it on toast. Come on Brits, we can be more bonkers with butter than that, can't we? Oh wait, for a while we did bury it in mud.

Dating back to the first century AD, those canny Brits and Irish would pack wooden barrels full to the brim with butter, and then bury them in peat bogs for years and years and years, so long in fact that they would often forget where they put them in the first place, which is so often the case when you want to put something nice aside for the grandkids. In 2016 Jack Conway shared with the world a 22lb block of butter that he'd unearthed from a bog in County Meath, Ireland, estimated to be more than 2,000 years old. It is uncertain if next to it he found a 2,000-year-old jar of Marmite, but one would like to think so. So why did our forefathers bury butter in bogs? History has forgotten, and we have absolutely no idea.

As BC clicked over into AD in the year 1 – and what a New Year's Eve party that must have been – history in general, and that of butter in particular, becomes a lot easier to follow on account of the number of people writing things down.

In the year 476 the Roman Empire found itself on the brink of collapse. Until now, Rome's ruling elite had decided that the purpose of butter was as a skin cream, and the idea of eating it would be like us chowing down on a tube of Germolene. Olive oil was to them the only civilised accompaniment to bread. Yet there were butter eaters out there. The barbarians.

The barbarians were considered uncouth and uncultured and really rather annoying as they were kicking the pants off Rome. With the final battle won, Rome sacked and the barbarians now in control, butter fast replaced olive oil as the go-to. Although this did much to increase the spread of butter, it did taint it as a lower-class food, and that stigma lasted throughout the Middle Ages.

Rome's demise complete, the butter-eating barbarians put down their weapons and became butter-eating peasants. However, the upper-class toffs of the time couldn't help themselves looking down on the peasants and their liberal use of butter, and considered them very seriously chavvy. In a bid to rise above the riffraff they limited their own intake of the yellow spread, and during Lent abstained completely. Which, it transpires, was more difficult than they'd given credit. You see butter is really rather scrummy, and Lent can last for forty-six long, long days. In the sixteenth century a petition was made to have butter permitted during Lent, and finally the Roman Catholic Church said, 'Okay, okay, for goodness sake, you can eat butter during Lent, happy now?' And the toffs went, 'Yes, thank you.'

This is an important moment because it meant butter was recognised as a necessary staple of life. You'd think they'd all celebrate this; they'd even devised a better way of making butter that didn't involve an animal skin filled with cream and hung from a branch and swung for half a day, which until then had been all the rage, and replaced it with a churn. But no, oh no, no, no. That would be far too easy. So to keep things nice and complicated they introduced witches, superstitions, and even Beelzebub himself, because if mankind knows anything he knows how to freak himself out and make life difficult.

Although churns had been kicking around for several millennia, it wasn't until the twelfth century that they really came into their own as a common object. Churns were small barrels with a stick, known as a dasher, poked in the top. The idea would be to fill the barrel with cream, and then either twirl the dasher or thump it up and down until butter was made. It was *really* hard work, and would take hours, so obviously men delegated it as a woman's job.

However, making butter is not an exact science. One day you might get a really good yield, the next not so good, or on a really bad day you might not get any butter at all. There are lots of reasons for this, such as ambient temperature, the temperature or quality of the cream, humidity, or even the state of the churn itself, the list goes on. But canny butter makers decided to ignore all of that science malarkey and put it down to witchcraft. If you couldn't make butter, it was because you'd gone and got yourself a butter witch. Pesky things.

But it didn't stop there. Even before the witch could think of infiltrating the churn, there were fairies out to get your cattle and contaminate the milk so the cream you got from it was doomed, doomed I say, right from the start.

The trick was to sing a few songs while milking and, once done, place a needle in the milk. Or, if things got totally out of hand and you were forced to up the ante, you dropped a red hot horseshoe into the churn. It's a shame we gave up these charming old traditions. However, I must add a serious caveat that if you do have trouble with your butter making and suspect the foul play of witchcraft, these incantations were practised by highly qualified Wise Women and should not be attempted by the layperson, as goodness only knows what might happen if you're not totally au fait with banishing spells.

In the 1800s, the industrial revolution, that bit in history known to schoolchildren across the globe as the dullest period in human evolution, engulfed even butter making. Until then just about all butter had been made on farms and sold to the local community. But industrialisation snatched it away and widened it out to the masses. Sure, this would have hit the farmer's pocket hard, but you imagine the poor farmer's wife who was spending half her day stooped over the churn working the dasher for all she was worth was secretly rather pleased. Around this time history also reports a sharp decline in the previously lucrative business of butter witch incantations.

With mass-produced butter in its infancy, but certainly taking hold, homemade or farm-made butter made a new status claim by reinventing the churn. You see, farmers were on a back foot. Butter had been a rather nice little earner, and now that income stream was getting squeezed. To thwart this, it was the farmers themselves who turned their attention to the churn. Virtually unchanged for hundreds of years because, well, it's only the women and children who have been making butter and suffering, and you know what whingers they are. Men suddenly decided there might be an easier way to make butter after all! Who knew? In just a few years, more than 2,500 patents were submitted for faster, easier, more efficient churns by pleased-with-themselves men and their exasperated wives.

One pleased-with-himself man was Nathan Dazey. In the early 1900s, Dazey, from Fort Worth, Texas, brought out a rather sexy glass churn that turned the heads of many. It was a small gadget that sat on the worktop, looked great and was marketed as 'The Premier Two-Minute Butter Machine'. For the housewife, it was a godsend. It's worth making a mental note the next time you're rummaging around a flea market or bargain-hunt-

ing your way through a boot sale, that early Dazey churns now fetch thousands at auction, but if you're tempted, be sure it's an original as there are a lot of fakes out there. At its peak, Dazey was turning out hundreds of churns each week, although the Great Depression saw demand slump. But through tenacity and a need for churns that never completely died out, the company kept going, and the Dazey churn is still being made today.

WHAT IS BUTTER ANYWAY?

Butter is the fat globules in milk. That's it. That's all it is. The trick to obtaining butter from milk is to separate those fat globules from the liquid. To do this, you need to beat them out. Smash them. The more vigorous you are, the quicker you'll knock the solids out of solution. The name for this process is churning.

Churning breaks down the chemical composition of milk into the component parts of fats and liquid. Once split, the fats will bond together and form butter, while the liquid will form fat-free buttermilk.

But churning milk to try and make butter would have you worn out long before you'd get anything worth putting on your toast. The trick is to start not with milk, but with cream. Double cream.

To give you an idea of what we're looking at here, most of us have at some time over-whipped double cream. You look in the bowl expecting to see firm white peaks but instead find it's gone sloshy and grainy. Well that's the start of butter! Carry on for a couple more minutes and you'd have been there.

So maybe before we start looking at butter we should spend a moment or two on the raw ingredient, milk.

The raw material – milk

All female mammals produce milk in order to feed their young, known as lactating. The length of lactation may vary, not only between species, but also between individuals, and the component parts and trace elements may also vary, depending at which point during her milking cycle the milk is analysed.

However, in general terms, raw (unpasteurised) cow's milk is likely to contain:

- 85–90% water
- 3–6% lactose (milk sugars)
- 3–6% fat
- 3–5% proteins
- 0.5–1% vitamins, minerals and salts

Just about all milk is processed before it hits the shelves. Pasteurisation is the process of rapidly heating the milk for a short time to kill off any harmful bacteria. It is then sold as whole (full cream) milk, with about 4% fat, or further processed into semi-skimmed, skimmed or fat-free milk.

If left to settle, the part of the milk that contains the most fat – the cream – will rise to the surface (these days it's usually removed using a cream separator). There are a whole host of factors that influence the fat content of the cream, including the breed, diet and age of the cow, but it's generally between 30 and 55% fat.

It is thought that around 90 per cent of the world's milk comes from cows, mainly because they're so prolific. A cow's full udder will hold between 10 and 20 litres of milk, and she will produce about 50,000 litres in her lifetime.

While cow's milk is the most common, other choices are increasingly widely available. For example:

- Goats' milk – considered to be slightly better for you than cow's milk because the fat globules are considerably smaller and therefore easier for the body to digest. It takes about 20 minutes for the body to absorb goats' milk as opposed to an hour for cow's. Goats' milk also contains more calcium, more vitamins and more potassium, and less lactose (sugar).
- Dairy-free milk – it's fair to say that dairy-free milk has come a long way in recent years. Viable options now include almond milk, soy milk, rice milk, coconut milk, hemp milk and oat milk.

For butter making, we will predominantly be looking at dairy milk. However, I have included some dairy-free and vegan options. One of the main reasons people opt for dairy-free milk is to avoid lactose. Lactose intolerance is a growing problem, and for sufferers can be a real issue.

LACTOSE INTOLERANCE

This is a partial or total inability of the body to digest the sugars (lactose) found in milk. The symptoms are pretty uncomfortable, though seldom dangerous, and sufferers are advised to seek medical help. In extreme cases they may need to avoid dairy altogether.

However, in many milder cases it is worth exploring different types of milk. For instance, you may find that goats' or sheep's milk can be consumed with little or no ill effects as they contain far less lactose than regular cow's milk.

Butter is low in lactose, and ghee (see page 16) is lactose-free, so there should be no need to avoid these if your symptoms are mild.

Please note that allergies are different from intolerances, and people with milk allergies will need to avoid all dairy products, including butter.

If you have any concerns, ask the advice of your medical practitioner.

Defining butter

Butter is not easy to define. Depending on the temperature it can be solid or liquid. The taste can be deep and rich and creamy, or light with very little flavour to speak of. The spectrum of colour runs from orangey-yellow to white. Yet despite these inconsistencies, every single one of us knows exactly what we mean when we say the word butter.

As we now know, butter is a product made from the solid compounds in milk. For home butter making, it would be more accurate to state that butter is made from the solid compounds in double cream. Those compounds are fats, proteins, vitamins and trace elements.

To give you an example of how butter is made up, the following is an average taken from a standard 250g pack of cow's butter:

- 1,800 calories
- 200g fats
- 2.5g protein
- 1g omega-3
- 5.5g omega-6
- Water
- Vitamins A, D and E

Now let's put some of that into perspective. One tablespoon of butter has the same number of...

- ...calories as half a packet of crisps
- ...fat as 30g of almonds
- ...protein as a single egg white

The colour of butter, from a deep sunny yellow to almost white, is a direct consequence of the food the mammal eats. Animals such as cows that eat low down, munching on grass and plants that are high in beta carotene, will produce a yellow butter. However, goats, who are browsers and prefer their food source on branches and bushes, will produce a much whiter butter, with less beta carotene. Beta carotene is converted in our bodies into vitamin A. It is also the reason carrots are orange.

The nutritional facts

Opinions sway even amongst experts over the health-giving properties of butter. There are certainly elements within butter that are healthy. But then again, at 80% fat there are also things that aren't. However, it is pretty much accepted by the majority of nutritionists that eaten in sensible proportions, and as part of a healthy, balanced diet, butter isn't bad for you and can actually offer significant benefits.

The reason there used to be such controversy over butter is because it's so complex, and it took scientists yonks to work out how it affected our bodies. Today, thank goodness, we're getting a handle on it.

However, having said that, you first need to understand that not all butter is the same, and therefore the health benefits will also differ. For dairy butters, how the animal has been cared for, its diet and wellbeing will all significantly affect the quality of the milk it gives, including the vitamin content. This is ridiculously obvious to any woman who has breastfed her baby

and had to look after her own diet while she did. When you buy butter, buy the best you can afford. Preferably one from a single farm where the animals are free-range and happy. And the same goes for cream when you come to source that for your own butter making.

Now, the complexity of butter. Let's first look at that 80% fat, and DON'T PANIC! Not all fats are bad for you, and some are essential for a healthy life. On average butter is likely to contain more than 400 different fatty acids, of which:

- 65% are saturated fats
- 30% are monounsaturated fats
- 3% are polyunsaturated fats
- 2% are trans fats

Don't forget, these are percentages of the fats within butter, not butter itself. What's more, scientists now know that there are many types of saturated fats, several of which have positive health benefits. Butter from grass-fed cows has a higher level of omega-3 fatty acid, and the trans fats in butter occur naturally and are credited with protecting against various illnesses.

In addition butter also contains a plethora of essential vitamins, including vitamins A, D, E, B12 and K2.

Trace elements include selenium, iodine, zinc, copper, manganese and chromium.

MAKE YOUR OWN BUTTER

Various studies set out to show that butter will help with everything from sexual performance to preventing arthritis, and while it's fair to say there is little fact-based evidence to support these claims, especially in the small quantities of butter eaten as part of a healthy diet, it does put a smile on your face as you butter your toast.

CHOOSING WHICH CREAM TO USE

So we now know that making butter is the art of extracting fat from milk. In order to do this, you need to start with milk that has the highest percentage of fat you can possibly lay your hands on. Today, we call this double cream (in the USA it's called heavy cream). But with so many varieties of double cream available, which should you choose? For simplicity here we're only going to be looking at cream from cow's milk. We'll explore some of the most interesting alternatives on page 45.

Let's start by looking at your bog-standard tub of double cream. This would be produced along with your milk. A herd of cows is milked on the farm and a tanker arrives, collects that milk and drives it to a central processing plant – where it joins the milk from other farms. So your double cream could have elements from hundreds, if not thousands of different cows. Nothing wrong with that, *but,* the smaller the herd – especially when we start looking at different breeds of cows – the more intensely flavoured and more gorgeous your cream, and resulting butter, will be.

In the UK the breed of cow that everyone knows produces milk that's extra thick and creamy is the Jersey. Caramel-coloured body with eyes the size of dinner plates and eyelashes most girls would kill for, the Jersey cow is a treasure, and the cream is deep, thick and very yellow. Jersey double cream is perfect for your butter making.

It's all about condensing down the pool from which your cream is taken, so cream from a single breed of cow, such as the Jersey, is good, or from a single farm; found mostly in speciality shops, farm shops or online, you may have seen the tubs that state, 'Double

cream from Fred's, the farm 100 yards down the road that way,' or something similar. Sure, you're going to pay a little more because it's more expensive for them to produce, but it will be worth it and you will certainly taste the difference.

Ultimately, it wouldn't get any better than to get cream from just one, happy, well-looked-after cow. From the point of view of health, taste, animal welfare, that is the goal.

But we need to be realists here, and the chances are that's not going to happen, so I've produced a leader board of double creams for your butter making:

- Family house cow
- Single farm
- Single breed, such as the Jersey cow
- Generic double cream

In summary, when seeking out the double cream you want to use for your homemade butter, get the best you can afford.

Conversely, we now need to talk about cream to avoid, either because it won't churn or the yield is so small it's not worth the effort. These include:

- Single cream
- Whipping cream
- UHT or long-life cream
- Clotted cream

I churned a pot of single cream (18% fat) for 20 minutes at high speed without a hint of it turning into butter; the same size pot of double cream (53% fat) made butter in less than 5 minutes.

MAKE YOUR OWN BUTTER

UHT, whipping cream and clotted cream are all produced using heat and therefore won't work.

I have also tried churning both crème fraiche and soured cream, but after 20 minutes at high speed there was no discernible difference from the product I started with.

THE TOP FIVE TYPES OF BUTTER

As you would imagine with butter being such a universally loved food and found everywhere from the most revered restaurants to the humblest homes, and across every continent of the world, there are many varieties. Some of them are subtle regional variations, others have a hint of 'scorpion in the bottle of tequila' about them.

Generally speaking, however, there are five main types of butter: raw butter, sweet cream butter, cultured butter, clarified butter and ghee.

Raw butter, also known as farmhouse butter or natural butter, is not found much these days, and is made by taking raw (unpasteurised) milk straight from the cow and churning the 'top of the milk' into butter. Nothing added, nothing taken away.

Plus side: rich, creamy buttery taste
Down side: short shelf life

Sweet cream butter, or commercial butter, is what you'd recognise on any supermarket shelf across Britain, Europe and most of America. It is made from milk that has been pasteurised to reduce the number of potentially harmful pathogens.

Plus side: longer shelf life
Down side: milder, softer flavour

Cultured butter, predominantly found in France and a number of other European countries, this is made by adding a culture (live bacteria) to the milk. This converts the sugars into lactic acid, similar to the beginning of the cheese-making process, hence the slightly acidic, cheesy taste.

Plus side: strong taste and higher fat content, perfect for speciality breads and pastries

Down side: takes a bit of getting used to

Clarified butter is butter that's been cleaned up by removing milk solids and water. This is done by gently heating the butter until it melts, and then leaving it to cool. Once cool, a crust of the whey proteins and impurities will form on the top and can be removed. The result is a purer butter that does not need to be kept in the fridge and can be heated to a higher temperature without burning.

Plus side: longer shelf life even without refrigeration; good for frying

Down side: when making small quantities, the process can be quite wasteful as a proportion of the butter is skimmed off and discarded

Ghee is clarified butter, and then some. Originating in India, this butter is gently heated for between 45 and 60 minutes, removing the water, whey proteins and impurities. The water evaporates off and the impurities fall to the bottom, so the ghee can simply be poured through muslin into a separate container. Almost 100% butterfat, clear and gorgeous with a soft nutty flavour, it is used extensively in Asian and Middle Eastern cuisine.

Plus side: many advantages, including high smoke point (it can be heated to a higher temperature than clarified butter without burning), complex taste, lactose free

Down side: you will want to cook everything in it.

SALTED OR UNSALTED, THAT'S THE QUESTION

And it's a good one. Should we be using unsalted butter because it's better for us? Does it taste better? Why do most recipes call for unsalted butter? In fact, what's the point of salted at all? Shouldn't we just go unsalted all the way and be done with it?

Oh, if only it was that easy – and the answer is no, by the way, we shouldn't go unsalted and be done with it. Each has its own place. Of course, if you prefer one to the other, then that's fine. But broadly speaking salted is for your bread and sandwiches, while unsalted is for cooking and baking.

While it is true that salting anything will increase its shelf life, in the percentages added to butter the effect is minimal. To have any real effect the amount of salt you would need to add would make it unpalatable.

Salted butter For many chefs and home cooks, a good sea salt is the most important ingredient in the kitchen. Salt is a universal flavour enhancer. It will make sweet things taste sweeter, savoury more savoury, mask bitterness and boost umami. Salted butter in a sandwich or on toast lifts it from black and white into full techno colour with surround sound and a chorus line of girls doing the can-can.

Unsalted butter Mainly used in cooking and baking so the chef can control the seasoning that goes into each dish more precisely. However, unless you're going for a Michelin star, if you're halfway through a recipe and find it calls for unsalted butter and you only have salted, use it and just reduce the salt elsewhere.

DID YOU KNOW...?

- France is the biggest consumer of butter per capita. Germany is second. The UK is 16th.
- *Butter* is the title of a 2011 comedy film starring Jennifer Garner, about a butter sculpture competition.

- Butter was first added to popcorn in America in the 1950s.
- During the Second World War, in the UK butter was rationed to 2oz (57g) per person per week.
- In the 1970s, an over-production of butter in Europe gave rise to the phrase 'butter mountain'.
- In Tibet, intricate figures are carved out of butter and used in Buddhist rituals.
- Cocoa butter is not butter at all, but the oil extracted from the cocoa bean and used to make chocolate and cosmetics.
- Afternoon tea was first served in about 1840 by Anna, the seventh Duchess of Bedford, who got into the habit of asking for bread and butter as an afternoon snack for herself and her well-to-do friends.
- Butter is one of New York's most popular restaurants.
- The word 'butterfingers' was coined by none other than Charles Dickens in *The Pickwick Papers*, published in 1836.
- In 1926 Louis Armstrong recorded the jazz classic 'Butter and egg man', which was slang for a man new in town and flash with his cash.
- Butterflies are so called because it was believed the witches that took their shape stole butter.
- India produces 185,000 tonnes – the weight of some of the world's largest cruise ships – of ghee every year.
- Science has proved that the old wives' tale about a slice of bread and butter dropped will invariably land butter side down, is, in fact, true.
- In the world of snowboarding, 'butter' is a trick turn. Yeah dude.

CHAPTER 2

Making butter

This is where we're going to get busy. I like to switch my phone off, turn the radio up and make sure I'm not going to be disturbed. It's a little 'me time', when the rest of the world can give me a bit of space. The first time you make butter, you're going to want to give yourself forty minutes: ten minutes to set up, twenty minutes to make it and another ten to clean down. Afterwards, and as soon as you realise how easy it is, you'll be churning out butter in a fraction of that time.

In this section we'll go through, in easy stages, exactly how to produce your very own butter. Once upon a time this would have involved a large wooden churn and some backbreaking work, but thankfully these days we have newfangled things like electricity and food mixers.

There are many different approaches to making butter, some of them so complicated it makes you want to reach for a glass of wine just to cool your brain down while you think of them. But the method we're going to look at is the simplified way. It's butter making stripped down to its most basic essentials, sort of a *Full Monty* for butter, only with slightly less screaming involved. It's fast, fun and do-able in any kitchen.

As with anything, there are tips and tricks involved that have evolved over many years of butter making. These I'll happily share with you, and you'll see they are very practical. Some of the tips they swore by in years gone by, such as putting a needle in the cream before you start or using a dead man's hand to stir the cream, are entirely optional.

So, dairymaids and dairy dudes, let's roll up our sleeves and perform some alchemy.

GETTING STARTED

Keep in mind that a whole host of factors, such as the fat content of the cream, the temperature of both cream and your kitchen, humidity, may cause the yield to vary.

> **To make approximately 300g of butter and 180ml of buttermilk, you'll need:**
> 500ml double cream at room temperature
> Salt (optional)
>
> *Equipment*
> Food mixer with mixing paddle
> Tea towel
> Wooden board
> Scotch hands (butter paddles), or 2 wooden spoons

Churning

Nice clean surface to start with, and I'm living in a static caravan (while I'm building a house) with a kitchen work surface you can measure in nano-millimetres, so no moaning you haven't got enough space.

The cream. You want it at room temperature. If it's a scorching hot day, or conversely the igloo in which you live feels a bit nippy even to you, you might want to adjust the cream, but as a rule of thumb anything between 10 and 20 degrees will be fine.

My food mixer is Auntie Eileen's old Kenwood that she left to me. It dates back to the 1960s and is still going strong. The mixing attachment for butter making on a Kenwood is the K blade. Other makes and models have their own, but you want the mixing attachment, NOT the whisk or balloon as it will be a real faff to get the butter out of it at the end – not impossible, but definitely a faff.

Tip your cream into the mixing bowl, and set the machine going. At this stage, forget churning and think of it as whipping cream. Whip it until you'd be more than happy to dollop it on top of a bowl of strawberries, and then keep going. Overwhip it. It will start to go grainy.

Grab your tea towel and be ready with it.

The next stage on from grainy is a consistency resembling scrambled eggs. At this point, if you have a build-up of cream stuck to the sides of the bowl, stop the machine and use a spatula to push the cream down into the mixture. Then set the machine going once more.

Now, this is really important. Place the tea towel over the machine so it covers any gaps: it's going to splash, and not only you but your entire kitchen will get drenched in buttermilk.

So you've seen the mixture turn to scrambled egg consistency and you've covered it with the tea towel. Now listen. You'll hear it mixing, mixing, mixing, then suddenly you'll hear a *thwack, thwack, thwack*. Stop the machine! Turn it off. You're done.

Woo-hoo, we've made butter!

Separating the butter and the buttermilk

With something of a flourish, remove the tea towel.

That *thwack, thwack, thwack* sound you heard was the noise made when the cream splits into butter and buttermilk. The buttermilk has a watery consistency while the butter is, well, butter, and when it beats around in the machine it splashes the buttermilk.

The butter will have gathered around the mixing attachment, which is why you don't want to use a whisk. If you did use a whisk, don't panic, it's just awkward trying to get the butter out, but with a little patience and some choice swearwords, it's do-able.

Nothing is wasted, so before you start getting too excited about the butter, pour the buttermilk into a bowl, cover it with some clingfilm and pop it into the fridge to deal with later (see page 36).

Now the fun really begins.

Washing your butter

Run your clean hands under cold water for a moment or two to cool them down, and then pull the butter off the attachment. It should feel squidgy, like slightly softened butter, but should stay in one clump. If there are any rogue bits, stick them on like putty.

Scrunch your butter into a ball. As you do, you will see a fine white liquid popping out, almost as though it's sweating, and the more you press it, the more comes out. That's excess buttermilk, and we want to remove all of that because it's moisture that makes things go bad. The more moisture we can remove, the longer shelf life your butter will have.

The trick is to wash it. Literally, wash it.

Now you have a choice. You *can* get a nice bowl of bottled water that's been chilled in the fridge overnight, you might even have some ice in there, or you can do what I do, and run the cold tap.

Either way, take your butter and plunge it in the water, or place it under the slow running cold tap, and move it about. Being gentle all the while, squidge it, wring it, push and pull it until no more filmy buttermilk comes out and the water runs clear.

We're nearly there!

Patting your butter

As we've already said, it's moisture that makes things go bad. While washing will have removed some of the liquid, it won't

MAKE YOUR OWN BUTTER

have removed all of it. In order to get the last of it, we need to pat it.

Place your wooden board on the work surface and wet it. Then place your butter on to it. If you have Scotch hands or butter paddles, great. If not, get a couple of wooden spoons. Whatever you have, run them under the tap until they are thoroughly wet. Now pat, pat, pat the butter with the paddles/spoons.

Pat, pat, pat. Slap it, slap it, slap it. Little tiny volcanoes of buttermilk will spray out, and that's what we want, because by patting we're getting rid of any pockets of liquid buried within the butter. If your paddles/wooden spoons dry out, put them back under the tap.

Keep patting until nothing more comes out.

Salting

Salting is optional, but if you want to add salt to your butter, now is the time.

First, a word or two on salt. If you have a packet of generic table salt, take it out of your cupboard now, open your bin and chuck it away – have you no shame? Sea or rock salt only, darling. Flaked, ground or fine are all good; each will add a slightly different flavour. For something a little off the beaten track, why not try smoked salt?

Start with half a teaspoon of salt for each 250g of butter. This is less than you might find in most commercial butters, but you can always add more.

Evenly sprinkle the salt on top of the butter and cut it in. Cut and pat, turn the butter a quarter of a turn, cut and pat, cut and pat, turn the butter again a quarter of a turn, cut and pat, cut and pat, and repeat until the salt is evenly distributed throughout the butter.

As salt is added to taste, that's what we need to do. Taste it. Grab something bland like a cream cracker or a corner of bread. Put enough butter on so you can taste it. What do you think? Is that good? Does it need more salt? If so, add a little more and keep mixing. Or are you happy with it as it is? I'm guessing if you've got a smile on your face a mile wide it's okay.

FINISHING TOUCHES

Shaping your butter

Butter making is so creative, and you have many options along the way, but this is the first point where you really have a choice, and that is about what shape you want your butter to be. Think a little about what you're going to do with your fab homemade butter. Is it just to go on the side and be used as regular butter, or do you want to do something special with it and jazz it up a little?

Classic butter oblong

Using your damp butter paddles or wooden spoons, tap and shape the butter into an oblong block, wrap it in greaseproof paper and put it in the fridge to chill right down.

Cylinder

It always seems to be the posh butters that are shaped this way. Get your clingfilm and pull out a strip about 45cm long and lay it on the work surface in front of you.

Now get your butter and put it about a quarter of the way up. Take the leading edge of the clingfilm closest to you and lift it up and over the butter. Then roll the butter forward like you would a rolling pin. Gently give it some backward and forward movement until it's completely cylindrical. Don't worry too much at this stage about keeping the clingfilm tight as long as it's reasonably snug.

Once done, twist the open ends of the clingfilm so it pushes the butter up into the cylinder. Keep twisting both ends at the same time until it's firm. Chill in the fridge to keep its shape. Then remove the clingfilm and use a sharp knife to cut the two ends so they're flat, neat and tidy, and wrap in greaseproof paper.

Balls

These are such fun and very 1980s (although shaped balls of butter do seem to be coming back into fashion). Break out the leg warmers and shoulder pads and nip out for a quick perm. Spotify some Wham and go in search of the melon baller you haven't used since that epic '80s dinner party where you all got sloshed on Black Tower.

Chill the butter in the fridge and then, dipping your melon baller in a mug of hot water, push and twist it into your butter to make butter balls. Arrange them in a bowl, cover and store them in the fridge until needed.

Curls

Looks so impressive, but it's amazingly easy to do once you get the hang of it. The basic way is to take a cold, hard block of butter and place it in front of you. Then get a soup spoon, dip it in a mug of hot water and pull it towards you over the butter, scraping up a

curl of butter as you do. The trick is to keep the bowl of the spoon facing you, and almost vertical to the butter. It takes a bit of playing with, but trust me, it's worth the effort.

Alternatively you can get dedicated butter curlers, which can be ridged so your butter curls have waves, or smooth. The method is much the same: chill the butter block right down, dip your butter curler in a mug of warm water and draw it across the surface of your butter.

Presses

Put your butter between two sheets of greaseproof paper and roll it out with a rolling pin until it's about 1cm thick. Carefully slide it onto a clean chopping board and pop it in the fridge until it's cool and firm to the touch.

For this you're going to need some pastry/biscuit cutters. There are stacks of them in all different shapes and sizes, from love hearts to Christmas tree shapes. When your butter slab is cold and firm, simply remove the greaseproof and press out your desired shapes before arranging nicely.

Storing your butter

The last thing you want is to go to all the effort of making butter, only to find when you reach for it it's gone bad. Of course I'm guessing this book isn't your first ever introduction to butter, and you've most likely been happily keeping it for yonks, but with homemade butter that has nothing added to it other than a little salt to taste, and certainly no preservatives, we need to be extra vigilant to ensure it remains fresh for as long as possible.

Understanding what it is that sends butter off, the dos and don'ts, shoulds and should not's, is vital.

Four things to avoid

It's easy to forget just how susceptible butter is to outside influences, mainly because it appears so solid and robust. But it is a part of milk; okay, it's the solid part with the liquid removed –

MAKE YOUR OWN BUTTER

and it's the liquid that's the real carrier of harmful bacteria; remove the buttermilk and that's the breeding ground for most of your nasties taken out of the equation – but it's still a part of milk, and you would no more leave a glass of milk out on the side for a week and then drink it than you would leave your butter out, uncovered and exposed to the elements.

The good thing about butter is it will give you lots of clues if it's spoiling. The smell will change and turn sour. It will look shiny, even blotchy. Taste becomes sickly, and it will feel tacky. If you get a sense of any of these, bin it.

But what we really need to know is how we can prevent the butter turning bad in the first place. There are four main conditions that will accelerate the process of turning your butter rancid. These are moisture, light, temperature and air.

Moisture Water in butter is either free or bound. Bound means it's part of the compound, and free means drips; yes, that pesky buttermilk! And that's a problem because free water is a playground for microorganisms, whereas bound water is not. But it's not just internal, it's external too. Butter kept in a damp environment is a joyous place for bacteria and mould to live. The answer is to remove as much moisture during the manufacturing process as you can, and store your butter in a dry place.

Light Photodegeneration is the effect of natural or artificial light on butter. Lengthy exposure will spoil the outside by discoloration, vitamin loss and/or rancid taste. Always store your butter away from light.

Temperature The warmer the environment in which the butter is stored, the quicker the chemical reactions and enzyme reactions within it. These will greatly affect the butter in taste, appearance and smell, and will turn it bad at an accelerated rate. Keep your butter cool.

Air Oxygen is vital for life: for us, for animals, and for nasties. Microorganisms need air to thrive just as much as we do, and you don't want them thriving on your butter. Keep it wrapped, or in an airtight container.

So, how and where should you store your butter?

Refrigerator

It's hard to believe that fridges have only been around for the last hundred or so years. Can you imagine what a nightmare it must have been to keep things cold before then? Keeping your butter well chilled will keep it fresh for longer. Wrap it before you put it in the fridge as it can absorb strong flavours and smells, such as a cut onion or garlic.

Homemade butter will happily last 3-4 weeks in the fridge, or even longer if you managed to get all the buttermilk out.

The downside to keeping butter in the fridge is it's not spreadable.

Room temperature

Butter kept at room temperature has the advantage of being spreadable, but the lifespan may shorten considerably.

It's important to keep your butter well covered as it can be a sponge for rogue flavours, and butter left out while you cook your signature Friday night curry will likely spice up your toast the next morning. Keep the butter in a cupboard, preferably in its own container that is thoroughly washed and dried between replenishing.

Homemade butter, at room temperature, depending on how much buttermilk you managed to pat out of it, should last 2-3 weeks.

The caveat to all of this is, if the room temperature increases to such a point that your butter starts melting, put it someplace cooler. Butter that's liquefying will turn bad in a matter of days, and make a heck of a mess in your cupboard.

Freezer

Butter lends itself beautifully to freezing, and should be stored on a shelf in your freezer beside a loaf of bread and a carton of milk as your emergency rations. Knot it in a bag so it's airtight. Frozen butter will happily last a year. Defrost the butter at room temperature overnight.

Making it spreadable

Butter in its natural state is not spreadable when cold. Sliceable, yes. Spreadable, no. However, if you want it a little softer and less likely to tear holes in your bread as you try and smooth it across, you can make it so.

To achieve a softer consistency, you need to add oil. Be aware that while this is a neat trick to make your butter a little more user-friendly, you are changing the compound, and as such the flavour will alter slightly, along with the texture.

To make approximately 250g of spreadable butter, you'll need:
200g butter
100ml oil of your choice, but something bland like sunflower works best

Equipment
Food mixer or hand whisk

You can use any amount of butter, just scale up or down the percentages.

Leave your butter out so it comes up to room temperature, then roughly cut it into a dozen or so bits.

Put the butter bits in your mixing bowl and start the machine on slow. The process of mixing will soften your butter even more. Add the oil a slug at a time. Quite quickly you will see the butter slacken considerably.

Once all the oil has been completely mixed in, transfer the butter to a tub or jam jar. *Voila!* Spreadable butter.

Churning options

Churning is simply the word used to describe the process of beating up cream until the fat falls out of solution, and there are loads of different ways of doing that. I love the idea of sitting on the stoop (I'm not entirely sure what a stoop is, but it seems to be important that you sit on one) with an old-fashioned wooden churn and dasher and making butter the way it used to be done. I bet it adds something to the taste.

Today there are many churning options.

Butter churn

Authentic and fun, but time consuming, and you will need a considerable quantity of cream for it to work, possibly as much as 5 litres.

The churns themselves are wooden barrels that either stand upright and have a dasher sticking out the top, that needs to be vigorously banged up and down, or the barrel will lay on its side, mounted in a frame with a handle at one end so you can spin the barrel.

Both are backbreaking, and you're looking at investing a good morning's work to produce your butter. However, the length of time it takes to churn, the fact that it's being processed in wood as opposed to glass or plastic, along with the quantity you're working with, all have an effect and the butter you produce is utterly outstanding.

The downside is the cleaning, as you really have to clean and dry it well, and it won't fit in the sink.

Dazey churn

Now you're talking! In the absence of a food mixer, this is the way to go. A hand churn that will whizz out your butter in no time at all. Simple to use, quick and easy to clean.

Imagine a Kilner jar with a whisking attachment on the lid, so you've got cogs and a handle out to the side, and beaters inside the jar. As you turn the handle the mechanism works its way down inside the jar and the beaters spin at the speed you turn the handle.

Perfect for small batches, this was the original must-have kitchen gadget, and if you want to make your own butter, it still is.

Food mixer

Practical, quick and simple. If you already have one, great. If not, there are stacks of them on the market, and they're not expensive and well worth the investment. Just make certain you pick one with a mixing blade. The mixing blades are flat – on a Kenwood it's the K blade, so called because of the large K in the centre. Other food mixers have their own designs. Avoid using the balloon whisks as it's a real faff trying to get the butter out from the middle.

If you get the butter-making bug, the food mixer is undoubtedly the way to go, as it's fast, takes very little physical effort and a swift clean down.

Jam jar

Nice and clean with a tight-fitting lid. Half fill it with room temperature double cream and hand it to a small child to shake. It's hard work and takes ages, and will make you about as popular as the child catcher in *Chitty Chitty Bang Bang*. Or, if you happen to have two children in your kitchen, tell them this is science – turning a liquid into a solid. Give them each a jar, but include a ping pong ball in one jar to see if the extra surface area speeds up the process. Perfect for a rainy afternoon, and if nothing else you are making a memory.

Hand whisk

Do-able, but definitely a job to delegate. You will need a bowl, a hand whisk and a lot of muscle. Not for the faint hearted, or weak wristed. Go for small amounts unless you're going to hand it to someone to do for you and you're feeling particularly wicked.

Blenders are a no no Unfortunately they don't work. They are made to blend and not to beat or mix, and they just don't cut it.

Using a butter press

Butter presses are so beautiful, and are exactly what they say: a press put over a small pat of butter to create a shape. Generally made from wood, with more modern ones in plastic, butter presses have images in relief that when pushed down onto soft butter will shape it into that pattern.

The result is very flamboyant, not unlike a posh lady's brooch but made of butter. These are designed for individual pats, so you might have one on each side plate at a well-to-do luncheon or soiree. Typically they would show images of cows, plants, flowers or countryside, or the head and shoulders of a pretty girl meant to depict the dairymaid who churned the butter herself.

Antique butter presses are tremendously desirable and are normally snapped up from antique and curiosity shops – they make fabulous decorative items in big country kitchens propped up against the Aga when one has *Homes and Gardens* magazine down for a photo shoot.

Modern and plastic butter presses are slightly more affordable, though no less fun.

Using butter moulds

Very theatrical, butter moulds are a step up in size and shape from the butter press. Rather than prettifying individual pats, butter moulds are designed to create big and bold butter statements for blocks almost the size of a cat.

Of course they're ostentatious, but that's the point. It's way too easy to spend your life being humdrum and tasteful. There isn't one of us who wouldn't benefit from a bit of nuts every once in a while. Think about it this way, if you were throwing a dinner party for Liberace, Zsa Zsa Gabor, Elton John and Lady Gaga (and come on, who wouldn't want to be at *that* table?), that is how you'd present your butter. *'Could someone please pass me the butter Buddha? It's next to the cute little butter lamb. Beside the butter shoe. Darling, please don't hog the piano, we all want a turn.'*

With butter moulds, you're restricted only by your imagination. Search for butter moulds online and you can find pretty much anything, and any size from ahhh to *arrgh!*

To use a butter mould, chill it in cold, preferably iced, water for an hour or two, while you gently melt your butter. Drip dry the mould, then pour the soft, semi-melted butter in all the way to the top. When full, cover it and put it in the fridge overnight to set firm. Turn it out or, if your mould comes in two halves, turn them both out and assemble just before you're ready to present.

Personalising your butter with a stamp

Made popular in the days of farmhouse butter, where you'd actually go to the farmer's house to buy it, stamps were a way of branding the butter so everybody knew which farm it came from.

Today it's not that dissimilar, in that you are personalising your butter by imprinting something into the top. Stamps are for butter what a tattoo is for a bicep. It says, I'm an individual and this motif that I choose to share with the world is a piece of art that represents some facet of me.

Butter stamps can be wording, often something like BUTTER, PEACE, LOVE, HAPPY, or even the name of the restaurant in which you're sitting. They can be symbols, pictures, cartoons or Celtic patterns. Whatever you use says something about you as a person.

Normally made from wood with a handle running down to a flat-bottomed base, upon which the design sits, so when you stamp it that design is forced into the block of butter.

Using a pastry brush (or a corner of some kitchen paper) sparingly paint a little sunflower oil over your stamp. Take your block of butter and let it sit out at room temperature for an hour or so until it softens slightly. Then stamp the butter, using only as much pressure as needed to achieve the imprint.

Embracing the butter dish

So you've made the butter, shaped it and embellished it with a stamp or shape. What are you going to do now, wrap it in greaseproof paper or, worse, a wrapper you've saved from shop-bought butter? Come on, you can do better than that! What you need is a butter dish.

If you haven't had one before, it can be kind of scary and you may feel like you're turning into your grandma. That or you've suddenly been bumped up to middle class because everyone knows that money and butter dishes are a sure sign that you've made it in life. Either way, be brave and embrace the butter dish. Of course, if you already have one you'll be nodding your way through this section.

A butter dish is basically somewhere nice to keep your butter. Most often they will be a flat-ish plate upon which you sit your butter, and a bell-like cover that fits over it. They can be made from stainless steel – if you want to feel like you're having breakfast in a swanky hotel – ceramic, plastic or wood. They can be decorated so they're funky and borderline psychedelic, or staid and conservative. They can be rustic, ironic, chronic or demonic. There are cute ones, contemporary ones, retro ones and ones with polka dots. They're very individual.

Now here's the thing: you should change your butter dish at least twice a year. Think about it – you look at your butter dish umpteen times a day. It's one of the first things you see in the morning as you make breakfast, and one of the last things you see at night as you give the kitchen a quick tidy before bed.

So choose a butter dish to represent how you want to feel. If you want to feel upbeat and positive, go and buy one with big bold reds and yellows. If you want to feel reflective and mellow, buy one with muted blues. If you want to feel like a cow, buy one in black and white. If you want one to match your kitchen, go and get a life. Seriously, this is one thing that you can spend very little money on that will have a positive impact on your mood.

The joys of a butter knife

It's fair to say that in the 1600s dinner table etiquette was a bit rough around the edges, with people lounging back after a big meal and using massive knives to dig out any debris lodged in their teeth the way we might floss today, which inevitably led to some pretty horrific post-pudding violence. One minute you're asking someone to pass the port and the next it's all kicked off and one of your guests gets stabbed, which is so annoying and likely to ruin your best tablecloth with the bloodstain.

Deciding enough was enough, King Louis XIV of France banned all sharp-tipped knives from his table, hoping to reduce the number of people maimed and killed and improve dental hygiene, and I must say I've often done the same when it's my turn to have the family for Christmas. In their place he ordered flat round-tipped knives, or, as we call them today, butter knives.

Years down the line butter knives are all about function and beauty. Function because the blade of a butter knife is much wider and flatter than, say, a steak knife, and when you slice into your butter and aim to transfer it from the butter dish to your toast, it eliminates that wobbly, balancing, 'I hope I make it to the plate without dropping it on the worktop or the floor' thing we all do. And beauty because there are some

stunning butter knives. Ornate antique, shiny modern, or carved from wood. Like so much surrounding butter, it's very individual.

If you think that by not having a butter knife you're making a statement that you're a bit radical and windswept and interesting, you've got it the wrong way round. It's people *with* butter knives that stand out. But not just any old knife: make it special. Something that means something to you. Have a look around, you'll be amazed at what's available.

MAKING USE OF BUTTERMILK – THE BY-PRODUCT

The subject of buttermilk would make a book in itself. Buttermilk is an amazing by-product of butter, and in years gone by people swore by it as everything from a drink that was said to boost one's immune system, sense of wellbeing and energy – sort of the Red Bull of its day – to a hangover cure gulped down the morning after a heavy night. Young girls were encouraged to wash their faces in it to keep their skin young, soft and pretty. But it was most desired for cooking, and this is where it really comes into its own.

Today there are two types of buttermilk: traditional buttermilk and cultured buttermilk.

Traditional buttermilk This is the by-product of butter making. It's the liquid that remains once the fatty milk solids have coagulated into butter and, as such, is virtually fat free.

Fresh, it has a thin, watery consistency, with a cloudy colour and just a whiff of a milky scent; the taste is buttery to begin with but the aftertaste is watery.

However, leave it out for 36 hours at cool room temperature and it begins to ferment, as a result of the natural bacteria in the air; the process is similar to the fermentation of wild yeasts in some sourdough starters and cheese making. The buttermilk then thickens to the point that it resembles the viscosity of single cream. The colour will deepen to a yellow hue, the smell and the taste will become more pronounced with an acidic tang.

Cultured buttermilk Commercially made by adding enzymes, thickening agents and flavour enhancers to skimmed milk, which creates a sharp, acidic, thick liquid not unlike that of runny yoghurt. Cultured buttermilk is a popular ingredient in baking: when recipes call for buttermilk, it's cultured buttermilk they mean; in other words, shop-bought.

For the purpose of this book, when we talk about buttermilk, we mean traditional buttermilk – the liquid left over from your home butter making. To store your buttermilk, treat it as skimmed milk: keep it in a container in the fridge, or freeze for later use.

It is so good for you and is such a treat that we should spend a few moments thinking about how best to use it. Your options are to drink it or to cook with it. I guess you could also wash your face with it if you want to stay young and pretty, but you're probably better off nipping out to Lush.

Buttermilk as a drink

Straight up, fresh from the fridge, it is so refreshing, and it does feel rejuvenating, especially on a warm summer's day when you have a tendency towards lethargy.

Or spruce it up! Use it as a base for your smoothie or shake, or how about a hot chocolate using a couple of squares of organic 70% cocoa solids chocolate that you add to the warmed-up buttermilk and whisk until completely mixed. You can add a teaspoon of honey for sweetening or a tot of brandy for warming.

Buttermilk in cooking

This is where it really gets exciting. Buttermilk is unlike anything else you use in your cooking and baking. It puffs and lightens and adds flavour and texture. It can be a background or foreground ingredient, and it will make you turn a cartwheel in your kitchen when you taste the results. The following recipes are a few family favourites for using buttermilk.

American-style pancakes

Easy to make, these will take about an hour from start to finish and you will love yourself for them, as will your friends and family if you can bear to share.

MAKES 10-12 PANCAKES

150g self-raising flour
1 teaspoon baking powder
½ teaspoon salt
20g (homemade) butter, softened, plus a knob for greasing
220ml buttermilk
1 teaspoon honey (or caster sugar)
1 egg

1 Measure out the dry ingredients into a bowl.
2 Put all the wet ingredients, including the softened butter, in a jug. Carefully tip the wet into the dry and beat until smooth, then return to the jug.
3 Meanwhile, heat a non-stick frying pan on a medium heat, add a knob of butter, and when the butter is bubbling, pour in a circle of the batter. After about a minute you should see bubbles appear on the surface of your pancake. Using a spatula, turn the pancake and cook for another minute or two. The pancake should be golden brown on both sides.
4 Repeat until all the pancakes are cooked, stacking them as you go.

TOPPINGS
Add butter and honey or jam, maple syrup and crispy bacon, or your favourite topping, or for something extra special jump to the flavoured butters on page 56.

Blinis

A really nice alternative to boring old crisps, blinis make perfect nibbles. Being from Russia they should probably be topped with caviar and accompany a shot of ice cold vodka, but to be honest they work brilliantly with one of the new wave gins and some smoked salmon.

MAKES ABOUT 24 BLINIS

120g plain flour
7g pack fast-action dried yeast
175ml buttermilk
1 teaspoon honey (or caster sugar)
25g (homemade) salted butter, plus a knob for greasing
1 egg, separated

1 Measure out the dry ingredients into a bowl.
2 Warm the buttermilk and honey in a saucepan. Add half to the dry ingredients and mix well.
3 To the remaining buttermilk and honey in the saucepan, add the butter and warm until just melted. Pour it slowly into the mixture, beating all the while, until the batter is smooth. Add the egg yolk and continue beating until well mixed.
4 Whisk the egg white to soft peaks and fold it into the batter.
5 Heat a frying pan, add a knob of butter, and when it's good and hot carefully drop in spoonfuls of the batter, making rounds about the size of a tea-light.
6 Cook for 1–2 minutes on each side until golden brown. Leave to cool before adding your topping.

MAKE YOUR OWN BUTTER

Rich scones

Summer. Blue sky, the sound of a lawnmower somewhere in the distance and the smell of freshly cut grass in the air. And scones for tea. Come on!

MAKES ABOUT 12 SCONES

220g self-raising flour, plus extra for dusting
1 teaspoon baking powder
60g (homemade) salted butter, diced
1½ tablespoons honey (or caster sugar)
1 egg
140ml buttermilk, plus extra (or milk) to glaze
Clotted cream and strawberry jam to serve

1   Preheat the oven to 230°C/gas mark 8 and put a baking sheet in the oven to heat up.
2   Measure out the dry ingredients into a bowl. Add the butter and rub in until the mixture resembles fine breadcrumbs. Then add the honey or sugar.
3   Beat the egg into the buttermilk and tip it into the mixture. Mix to combine until you have a soft dough. Turn out onto a floured work surface and knead briefly – 1–2 minutes is fine.
4   Using a rolling pin, flatten to approximately 2cm thick. Using a floured pastry cutter (I use a 6cm diameter one) stamp out your scones, taking care not to twist the cutter or you won't get an even rise.
5   Place on the hot baking sheet and brush the tops with buttermilk or milk, taking care not to let the milk dribble down the sides. Bake for 12–15 minutes or until golden brown.
6   Transfer to a wire rack and leave to cool slightly.
7   To serve, split the scones in two and smother them in jam then clotted cream, or is it cream then jam? When they're served up smelling and looking this good I'm normally just a blur of dolloping, smothering and slathering and completely forget what's supposed to go first.

Buttermilk rolls

Light, fluffy and chewy, these are the Rolls Royce of bread.

MAKES 8 ROLLS

500g strong white bread flour
1 teaspoon salt
¼ teaspoon bicarbonate of soda
7g pack fast-action dried yeast
1 heaped teaspoon honey (or light brown sugar)
300ml buttermilk

1   Measure out the flour into a bowl. Looking down on it as a clock, put your salt at 12 o'clock, your bicarb at quarter past, your yeast at half past, and your honey at quarter to.
2   Make a well in the middle and pour in the buttermilk. Using your hand, bring the mix together until it forms a rustic ball. Turn out and knead for 10 minutes.
3   Put the dough back into the bowl, cover and leave it to one side until doubled in size. This will take roughly an hour.
4   Turn out again and knock back to dispel the air by kneading briefly. Divide the dough into eight equal pieces. Dough has an elasticity to it and will want to ping back into the shape it was, so leave it to relax for 90 seconds. Then roll each piece into a ball.

MAKE YOUR OWN BUTTER

5   Place them on a greased baking sheet with a couple of centimetres gap between each, so when they rise and bake they will be touching, known as kissing rolls. Dust lightly with flour, cover and leave to rise for another hour.

6   Always bake on a falling heat. Crank up your oven to the max and leave it for 20 minutes to really get up to temperature.

7   Put your rolls in. After 5 minutes, turn down your oven by 10 degrees.

8   After another 5 minutes, turn down your oven again by another 10 degrees.

9   After another 5 minutes, turn down your oven by another 10 degrees.

10 Last time, another 5 minutes, and down goes the oven temperature by another 10 degrees.

11 Take the rolls out when they're golden brown on top, and when you rip one off and tap the base it sounds hollow. Cool on a wire rack.

Soda bread

The beauty of this bread is there's no kneading! With a thick chewy crust, this loaf is delicious eaten warm from the oven with a hearty soup or hunk of cheese.

MAKES 1 LOAF

160g self-raising flour
160g plain flour, plus extra for dusting
½ teaspoon bicarbonate of soda
½ teaspoon sea salt
275ml buttermilk

1 Preheat the oven to 200°C/gas mark 6.
2 Measure out the dry ingredients into a bowl. Add the buttermilk and stir with a knife to make a dough.
3 Turn out onto a floured work surface and knead briefly, then form into a ball and place on a greased baking sheet. Flatten slightly with the palm of one hand, cut a cross in the top with a sharp knife, and dust with flour.
4 Bake for 30 minutes or until the base of the bread sounds hollow when tapped.
5 Serve while still warm, torn into chunks.

CREAMY ALTERNATIVES TO COW'S MILK

Although cow's milk is most common in butter making, it is far from your only choice. There are stacks of creamy alternatives you might like to explore. All female mammals produce milk, so in theory the animal kingdom is your playground. In practice, however, the thought of milking a stroppy hippopotamus is enough to put anyone off. Same goes for lions, tigers and anything with sharp teeth and a temper.

However, the list of domesticated animals is surprisingly long, and each one offers something different to your butter making, be it in taste or health. That said, the reason cow's milk butter is so common is because it's easy to get hold of, and the yield is good. As you start looking at other animals that changes. A sheep, for example, will need a week of milking every day to produce 250g of butter.

Online is a wonderful resource, and you can get pretty much any animal's milk or cream sent to you these days. But do make sure you're happy with the farm from which you're buying, and if possible, go and visit them. Make sure the animals are well cared for and free-range with plenty of natural grass and/or forage, because the quality and health-giving properties of the milk and cream will plummet if the animal is unhappy and malnourished.

Goats
Goat butter is very common, probably only second to cow's butter. Once the cream has been separated from the milk, the process of butter making is much the same for both. The main difference is in the colour, which, rather than an inviting creamy yellow, tends to be paler and resemble lard. To overcome this, many makers add a tiny amount of turmeric to give it a yellow tint. As all milk derives a high percentage of its flavour from the diet of the animal, it is highly advisable to avoid making butter from the milk of goats who have been anywhere near cabbages, or

bizarrely vanilla, which *really* bring out the goatiness. If not very fresh indeed, goats' milk butter can taste the way a billy goat smells.

Sheep

Easy to digest and high in vitamins, calcium and protein, this sweet milk can be made into butter, and is gorgeous! The downside is it would on average take a week of milking a sheep to produce enough cream for a 250g pat of butter. That aside, the high fat content and small fat globules make it tasty and easily digestible, even to many who may find themselves lactose intolerant (always seek advice from your medical practitioner), lending it a reputation of being 'healthy' butter. If you've ever been anywhere near a sheep and know how dopy and spooky they are, spare a thought for the poor sap tasked with milking them.

Water buffalo

Chances are you're already a confirmed fan of water buffalo cheese and will instantly be able to imagine what their butter would taste like, because mozzarella cheese is made from buffalo milk. Surprisingly, despite the cheese being so mainstream, water buffalo butter is still a speciality and is yet to catch on. It has a higher vitamin and fat content than cow's milk, but when churned into butter is not yellow, but white, and would lead you to believe that some of the goodness derived from beta carotene might be missing. However, the flavour is rich and creamy and definitely worth a try.

Yak

One of the earliest types of milk to be turned into butter, yak butter is still, after thousands of years, a food staple for the herding communities across China, India, Mongolia, Nepal and Tibet. Yak's milk is white, and not pink as some believe, with a high fat content making it ideal for butter making. The milk is said to be quite heavy, with a clean and mild flavour. The resulting butter is not one for your toast or sarnies, but is used extensively in tea, and a Tibetan herder might get through 40 cups a day. See page 90 for Yak butter tea recipe.

Moose

The milk from the female moose (also known as elk) is high in butterfat – more than twice that of cow's milk – and therefore lends itself beautifully to butter making. However, before I get into my stride on this, be aware that moose milk is *really* hard to get hold of unless you live in Russia, Sweden or Canada. In Canada, moose milk is a traditional alcoholic drink with strong links to the Canadian Armed Forces. Moose cheese can fetch in excess of 1,000 dollars a kilogram, and the butter, where available, isn't that much cheaper. The reason it's so expensive is partly the short milking season, only three months of the year, and also because the milk is said to be very beneficial: the story goes that in some parts of Russia they give it to hospital patients as a cure.

Reindeer

Massively high in butterfat, almost five times that of cow's milk, reindeer milk is a speciality in the Arctic and sub-Arctic. The problem is the quantity of milk they give, which can be less than a mug full a day. To then churn that into butter is a lot of work for not much return, and it's not as if the flavour will blow your socks off, as by all accounts it's quite an acquired taste. That said, you can't help thinking that reindeer butter around Christmas would go down a storm.

Donkey

Donkey milk is not at all popular, which isn't a total shock when you find out it's also called ass milk. They could do with employing a publicist and maybe think about changing the name. I don't think ass butter would catch on any better.

Horse

First off, having kept a crazy chestnut mare for twenty years, if you want to milk a horse, you're on your own. The golden rules would be approach with caution and make sure she's unshod. Arabian horse milk seems to be popular, and is said to have fruity undertones and a smooth finish. The problem seems to be the quantity a lactating Arabian mare will produce in a single milking, which is about a litre. However, the fat content is roughly the same as cow's milk, and the nutritional value is higher, so there's no reason why you couldn't make butter. That said, there are one million horses in the UK, and a quick search online reveals not a single retailer selling mare's milk for human consumption, so demand for your horsey butter is likely to be low.

Camel

While it is possible to make butter from camel's milk, the process is slightly more complex and involves an unwashed goatskin and a night in the Sahara desert beside a warm Bedouin campfire for optimum conditions. Churning must be started before dawn the following day, and managed by a man whose job it is to swing the goatskin with the milk inside for a number of hours until butter forms. Camel butter is illegal in America as quality standards cannot be guaranteed. In the UK camel butter is legal, but considered unlikely. Camel milk can be bought online, arrives frozen, and has a slightly salty taste.

DAIRY-FREE HOMEMADE BUTTERS

For some, dairy is not an option. Either through lifestyle choice, medical advice, or intolerance, negotiating a butter-free life can be a nightmare. So much of what we enjoy is flavoured with butter, from toast and sandwiches to lots of cooking, that it can feel overwhelming and majorly disheartening not to be allowed to eat it. But it needn't be. There are options, and they're so good you'll feel great and still be able to eat all your favourite foods.

Exactly the same arguments apply to dairy-free butter as they do to regular butter. Sure, you can go out and buy some mass-produced tub or bar of something off the shelf, and that has its place in our busy lives, but that's far from your only choice. Most of us would agree that the cleaner, more natural and less processed the food we put into our bodies, the better it is for us and the better we'll feel. Start shovelling in additives, flavour enhancers, stabilisers and preservatives every day and it kind of negates that desire for a healthy alternative diet that turned you away from dairy in the first place.

The answer, of course, is to make your own. By being a little creative, there is absolutely no reason why you should miss out on anything.

Coconut oil

There is some debate over the health benefits of coconut oil, depending on how you feel about saturated fats, as it has a much higher content at 82% than dairy butter at 65%. As part of a balanced, healthy diet that's not necessarily a worry, but it might be worth some further investigation if weight loss or heart condition is something that concerns you.

The high smoke point and the fact that it's solid at room temperature make coconut oil a great all-round butter substitute. Perfect for frying, greasing pans and some baking as a direct replacement for butter.

Nut and olive oils

There are loads, and I'm sure you'll have a favourite. They work really well in baking, especially when the recipe calls for melted butter. Obviously oils such as peanut (groundnut) oil and sesame oil have strong flavours of their own that will shine through in the finished product, while others such as vegetable oil are more neutral.

A straight substitution of oil for butter will tend to make your cake denser, so it's worth playing with the recipe until you're happy with the result.

Apple sauce

Especially good as a butter replacement in cakes as it keeps them moist and scrummy, and is best friends with berries and citrus.

Apple sauce is equally good with cheese on toast, in cheese sandwiches, etc. But for goodness sake, don't buy your apple sauce – we're trying to be healthy here. Make your own. Seriously, it takes no time at all, and you're also in control of any sweetening as many shop-bought sauces will have sugar added, which will affect your baking.

To make your own apple sauce, simply take a Bramley apple and peel, core and chop it. Put your apple chunks in a saucepan, add a tablespoon of water, and heat gently until soft. Mash with a fork. Store in a jam jar in the fridge.

Mashed banana

For cakes, breads, biscuits, muffins, simply swap the quantity of butter for the same of mashed banana. Because of the sweetness in bananas, reduce the sugar in the recipe by 25 per cent, and halve the number of eggs. Cooking time will also need to be adjusted: start looking at your baked goods at the three-quarter point – so if the recipe says bake for 20 minutes, get ready to take them out after 15 minutes.

As always, be prepared to play with the recipe until you get it spot on. When baking, bananas clash with berries and citrus and you should instead use apple sauce.

Mashed avocado butter

Dolloped on a hot jacket potato, oozing out of a tuna sandwich, this butter replacement is so tasty, and so good for you. Fast to make and keeps well in the fridge.

Flesh of 1 ripe avocado
Juice of ½ lemon
1 teaspoon Dijon mustard
Pinch of salt
Pinch of sugar
2 tablespoons olive oil

1 Add everything except the olive oil to a blender and start mixing. Drizzle the olive oil in slowly until thick and sumptuous.

Vegan butter

So far we have looked at butter substitutes: things you can use in place of butter. But sometimes you need that taste of butter and nothing else will do. For times like this, either because of the way it feels in your mouth or because you're cooking something special and you just don't feel that any of the  substitutes will quite hit the mark, the answer is to make your own vegan butter.

I have given two recipes for vegan butter. Both are quick and easy, and use standard vegan store cupboard ingredients. If you find you haven't got everything you need, a visit to your local health food shop should be all you'll need. Or of course a quick search online.

Vegan butter-ish

With a pleasant mousse-like consistency, this is great for anything where soft textured butter is needed, and lends itself well to adding strong flavours such as robust herbs, or garlic for garlic butter. Store in the fridge and it will last a couple of weeks.

200ml coconut oil, melted
4 tablespoons avocado oil
6 tablespoons aquafaba (liquid from a can of chickpeas)
2 teaspoons white wine vinegar
Pinch of salt
Pinch of turmeric

1   Combine the oils in a jug.
2   In a separate container, mix everything else using a stick blender. Still blending, add the oils a little at a time until it is all combined and you have a thick, gloopy, mayonnaise-like mix.
3   Transfer to a tub and put into the fridge to set.

Vegan butter-like

This has the same consistency, look and texture of regular dairy butter, and it's a pretty good substitute all round. For storage, treat as butter.

200ml coconut oil, melted
2 tablespoons vegetable oil
3 tablespoons unsweetened milk such as almond or cashew
(not soy, as it has a tendency to split)
1 teaspoon colourless vinegar such as white wine or apple
cider vinegar
1 teaspoon nutritional yeast
Pinch of salt
Pinch of turmeric

1 Combine the oils in a jug.
2 Add the milk and vinegar and mix.
3 Add the remaining ingredients and blend, using a stick
blender, until fully combined and smooth.
4 Transfer to a container and pop it into the fridge to set.

CHAPTER 3
....

Getting creative

Plain butter is only the start of the story. It's Harry Potter arriving at Hogwarts, the *Titanic* hitting the iceberg, or Elizabeth Bennett meeting Mr Darcy at the ball.

Up to now we've worried about keeping everything nice and clean with minimal washing up and a general sense of calm in the kitchen. Well that's about to get tossed out the window, along with your cup of tea and packet of biscuits, because butter-maids and butter-dudes, it's time to turn up the music and open the wine (please drink sensibly and take this as rhetorical if you've got to go and pick the kids up in half an hour) – it's time to have some proper fun with butter.

This chapter is about flavour, and cramming in as much as we can, so your pat of butter transforms from, 'oh, wow' into an atom bomb of taste exploding in your mouth. Butter is a brilliant vehicle for flavour. It carries it and enlivens it at the same time, and when you add butter to complementary dishes, it's like suddenly tasting in Super HD.

We want to excite, and thrill, and astonish with our butter, so included in this chapter are over one hundred different flavoured butters, each one with a serving suggestion that will really make it sing.

There are butter drinks, such as bulletproof coffee that's said to be a high-performance drink designed to make you think a little faster and give you an edge that many athletes, top CEOs and busy parents swear by. Then there are beauty products (don't go sniffy on me here, Cleopatra used milk and butter in her beauty regime and we're still talking about her looks two thousand years later), sauces, rubs and icing. It's not, 'if you can do it with butter, it's included,' because that would be boring. Instead, it's, 'if it can be done with butter *and* make a massive impact,' then it's in.

The hero, as always, is butter. If you can use your own homemade butter, it will taste and feel so much better. But I get it, life is busy and that's not always possible. If you want to use shop-bought, that's okay, but for goodness sake buy a decent butter, preferably local, preferably from a small farm.

My aim is to motivate you into action. To show you how easy and crazy fun playing with flavours around butter can be, and how, with a little knowhow, you can do things with butter that are truly outstanding.

Welcome to the not-so-dark art of butter gastronomy.

ACCESSORISING WITH FLAVOURED BUTTERS

Flavoured butters are ridiculously good fun, and will give a new and simple-to-do twist to all sorts of dishes, from old favourites to some more innovative ones that you might not have come across before. If a dish you've been cooking for yonks has begun to feel a bit samey, pep it up with a knob of flavoured butter. Butter melting over anything instantly makes it appealing, and that's even before the aroma of all the complex flavours hits you.

As this is a book on butter, the recipes and methods are all designed around getting the butter right. We want it to look amazing, taste fantastic and smell incredible. But what would be the point if that was all it was? This isn't art for the sake of art: we want to end up with something practical. Beside every flavoured butter is its best friend, so you will know which direction to take it, and exactly what it will go with.

I have broken this part into segments:

- Boozy butters
- Fishy butters
- From-the-garden butters
- Fruity butters
- Herby butters
- Meaty butters
- Nutty butters
- Smoky butters
- Spicy butters
- Sweet butters
- Wild butters

Each segment starts with a general conversation about the group before looking at proportions and methods of blending your flavourings and butter.

Presentation

First, however, we need to talk about how you're going to serve it. Food is *always* about how it looks. It has to look beautiful, end of story. When you have made your flavoured butter, spend a little extra time on shaping it so it looks nice; you can find some butter shaping ideas on page 24.

However, it's hard to beat a neat round. To achieve this, lay a length of clingfilm (approximately 30cm long) out in front of you. Spoon out your flavoured butter so it's about a quarter of the way up, then, taking hold of the edge of clingfilm nearest to you, lift it up and over the butter. Then roll the covered butter away from you, gathering the clingfilm around it as it goes. When you get to the end, roll it back and forth as though you were using it as a rolling pin. When it's nice and round, twist the ends tight up to the butter so you have a taut cylinder. Place it in the fridge to chill, and when you're ready to use it, remove the clingfilm and use a sharp knife to slice it into rounds (wheels).

Storage

Keep your flavoured butter in the fridge, wrapped in clingfilm. Use within three days.

All the flavoured butters – with the exception of fishy butters when they are made with previously frozen seafood – will freeze.

Boozy Butters

There are two distinct types of boozy butters – sweet and savoury. **Sweet** ones have added sugar and work well with spirits; they are used to accompany sweet things like cakes and fruits. **Savoury** ones are mostly based on wine or beer, using a reduction of the alcohol to concentrate the flavour; they accompany savoury dishes such as meat and fish. The good thing about flavouring butters with booze is that you don't need much of it to make a big impact, yet it looks and tastes so cool.

Method

For **sweet** butters, use 175g unsalted butter, 150g sugar (soft light brown or icing sugar) and 90ml spirit or liqueur. Beat the butter and sugar together until light and fluffy, and then add the spirit a dribble at a time while continually beating.

For **savoury** butters, heat 120ml wine, port or beer in a small pan with 2 pinches of fine sea salt, simmer until you only have 2 tablespoons left and then cool. Beat 85g unsalted butter and add the reduced alcohol a dribble at a time while continually beating.

Sweet boozy butter

Amaretto butter – with warm pear frangipane (almond paste) tart.

Brandy butter – the classic for Christmas pud and mince pies.

Rum butter – perfect on warm ginger cake.

Cointreau butter – on new season baked rhubarb.

Whisky butter – on stuffed apples.

Savoury boozy butter

Beer butter – on bread for a chip butty, served with a pint.

Champagne butter – on poached salmon.

Port or red wine butter – on grilled steak.

Bloody Mary butter (2 tablespoons of vodka and a touch of tomato puree, together with a drop of Tabasco) – mix with fresh breadcrumbs, stuff into hollowed-out tomatoes and roast.

Fishy Butters

These are perfect when you don't want the whole fish: perhaps you only have a small amount and need to eke it out; or you want to make nibbles to serve with drinks. These really add the wow factor to fish and shellfish dishes, and they're also great with eggs. They're easy to do and pack a punch far bigger than the sum of their parts.

Method

For crustaceans, you'll need the shells and/or heads of 8–10 prawns or crayfish, or 1–2 crabs or lobsters: poach the crushed shells/heads gently in 150g of clarified unsalted butter for 10–15 minutes. Push through a fine-mesh sieve, pressing to extract the flavour (if you like, you can whizz the butter and shells with a stick blender first), then chill.

Quite often when you buy prawns, lobster or crabs, you will find eggs (roe), which you can gently mix with a fork into softened unsalted butter.

For dried shrimps, grind them in a pestle and mortar before mixing into softened butter.

For meaty fish – such as salmon, anchovy, haddock – simply crush the prepared (cooked where necessary) fish into softened unsalted butter. The stronger the flavour of the fish the less you need to flavour the butter, so taste as you go.

For squid ink butter, using a fork, mix a sachet of squid ink into 85g of softened unsalted butter.

Fishy combinations

Crab and cayenne pepper butter – on muffins, or with a poached egg.

Crayfish butter – atop a seafood risotto.

Dried shrimp butter – to finish pan-fried scallops.

Lobster or prawn eggs butter – on any warm seafood.

Prawn head butter – amazing on grilled lobster tails.

Salted anchovy butter – on grilled or roast lamb.

Smoked salmon and lemon juice butter – on toast or warm blinis.

Smoked haddock butter – dolloped on eggs on toast.

Squid ink butter – dramatic finish to a seafood risotto.

From-the-Garden Butters

Vegetables and butter have been best friends forever, so bringing them together in a flavoured butter feels a natural thing to do. The vegetables bring colour, vibrancy and flavour to that lovely buttery finish.

Method

Roast the vegetables to concentrate their flavours. Use a stick blender to puree them with a little vegetable oil, cool, then fork into softened unsalted butter. With such a variety of flavour possibilities you'll need to taste as you go – remember that you can always add little more of the vegetable puree if you want a more intense flavour.

For nasturtiums and olives, chop them finely as for fresh herbs (see page 62) and gently fold into softened butter.

Veggie combinations

Beetroot and mint butter – for new potatoes.

Beetroot butter – for a gorgeous, sexy deep red colour, ideal for Valentine's day on a warm seafood salad.

Garlic (and parsley) butter – garlic bread, on grilled lobster, in baked potatoes – the list is endless!

Roasted garlic butter – for flat fish.

Nasturtium leaves, seeds and flower butter – for a hit of floral pepperiness on steak.

Green olive and lemon butter – on ravioli.

Pumpkin butter – topping a stack of American-style pancakes (see page 39) and bacon.

Tomato and basil butter – for chicken pasta dishes.

Red pepper butter – over a warm courgette and aubergine salad.

Sun-dried tomato butter (use the oil from the jar to blend the tomatoes to a puree and then mix with softened butter) – serve with pasta.

Fruity Butters

Citrusy, floral and sharp with killer looks, these butters are the celebrities of the flavoured butters. These are the ones that are photographed and seen in magazines because they look so good and taste amazing.

Method

For citrus fruits, beat the grated zest of the fruit (along with additional flavourings such as finely chopped ginger, chilli, herbs, or grated creamed coconut) into 100g softened unsalted butter, tasting to check the balance of flavours. For sweet fruity butters, first beat 50g icing sugar (or soft brown sugar) into 100g softened butter, then add the grated zest.

For apples, use a cooking variety such as Bramley, bake until soft, blitz with a stick blender and then heat in a pan on the hob to reduce and concentrate the flavour. Cool, and work into your softened butter.

For cranberries, use dried cranberries and very finely chop before mixing with softened butter.

For strawberries, simply mash them into sweetened softened butter.

Savoury fruity combinations

Apple butter – for a gammon steak.

Coconut and lime butter – on noodles and fish.

Cranberry butter – with leftover Christmas turkey.

Lemon and thyme butter – for fish.

Lime and coriander butter – over prawns.

Lime, chilli and fresh ginger butter – with chicken breast.

Sweet fruity combinations

Mandarin butter – on hot toasted fruit loaf.

Strawberry butter – for cupcakes.

Tangerine and stem ginger, dried fruit and brown sugar butter – in baked apples.

Tangerine and fresh ginger butter – for Christmas mince pies.

Herby Butters

For the cook, herbs come in two groups – soft and woody. The main difference when using them to flavour your butter is the quantity you need to use, as **soft** herbs are generally milder and would require, for instance, a tablespoonful to flavour 50g of butter, whereas **woody** herbs are more intense and would need only a teaspoonful for the same result.

Method

Using fresh herbs, pick the leaves, lay the leaves together and roll them into a tight cigar so they won't bruise and then chiffonade them – slice through the 'cigar' to make tiny ribbons. Gently fold into the softened butter until combined.

Using dried herbs, measure out the quantity you need and rub them between the palms of your hands to release the natural oils and aromas – which will help intensify the flavour – before beating into the softened butter.

To use capers – strictly speaking these are flower buds rather than herbs – simply rinse pat dry and chop finely.

To add onion or shallot, sweat the onion in a little butter until very soft and tender, leave to cool, then mash with the back of a spoon to make a paste; stir into the softened butter.

Herby combinations for soft herbs

Basil butter – as a dip for artichoke leaves.

Basil, pine nut and Parmesan butter – for pasta.

Caper butter – goes particularly well with monkfish or gurnard.

Chervil and dill butter – melting over plaice, dabs or any flat fish.

Fennel fronds and tarragon – loves steak.

Tarragon and juniper butter – melting over a thick venison steak.

Tarragon and red onion butter – with chicken.

Herby combinations for woody herbs

Lemon thyme butter – a happy match for chicken.

Mint butter – melting over a green vegetable risotto.

Oregano butter – on grilled aubergines and courgettes.

Summer or winter savory – perfect with pork.

Meaty Butters

Hands up if, as a kid, you used to have bread and dripping for tea on a Sunday night? Of course, now you're all grown up you'd never sneak a little just for nostalgia's sake while you're clearing up and the rest of the family are in the other room watching TV, right? Well, these meaty flavoured butters are a posh version you don't need to be closeted away to enjoy.

Method

For chicken skin, pancetta, bacon and pork crackling, bake until crispy, pat dry and cool. Grind to a fine powder. Mix into softened unsalted butter.

For meat glazes, collect the fat-skimmed juices left on the bottom of the pan after roasting a joint and add, with any additional ingredients, to your softened unsalted butter.

Meaty combinations

Crispy chicken skin butter – for scallops.

Crispy pancetta and roasted garlic butter – for mushrooms.

Pork crackling and summer savoury butter – for green vegetables.

Smoked bacon and sage butter – for pork.

Meat glaze and tarragon butter – beautiful with roasted tomatoes.

Meat glaze, shallots, red wine and parsley butter (soften the shallots in the meat glaze until very tender, then mash with the back of a spoon) – gorgeous on monkfish.

Nutty Butters

With nuts it's important to consider both the taste and the texture. As a rough guide, use one quarter of the weight of shelled nuts to unsalted butter.

Equipment
Nut cracker
Pestle and mortar for a crunchy finish
Spice grinder for a smooth finish

Method

Remove any shell and skin.

Toasting will increase the flavour by releasing the oils, so if you're looking for a real nutty hit, dry-fry the skinned nuts for just a minute or two. Do not be tempted to give them longer as the oils mean they easily scorch and go bitter.

Still warm from toasting, either crush in a pestle and mortar or pop through a spice grinder. Leave them to cool on a piece of kitchen paper.

Once cool, soften the butter and work in the nutty mixture until combined.

For coconut, I use a block of creamed coconut, finely grated.

Nutty combinations

Almond butter – best friends with white fish, such as plaice or sole.

Cashew nut butter – would sing with a robust fish, such as monkfish or gurnard.

Chestnut and chive butter – melting over a bowl of steaming Brussels sprouts.

Coconut, chilli and lime zest butter – works well with chicken.

Hazelnut, coriander and parsley butter – gorgeous on scallops, lobster or prawns.

Peanut butter – in thick, crusty bread sandwiches.

Pecan or walnut butter – melted until nut brown and used to dress a pear and blue cheese salad.

Smoky Butters

The earthy, slightly salty flavour of the smoke complements the rich butter and they lift each other like the best friends they are.

Equipment
Barbecue with a lid
Pro-Q smoker
Smoking (food safe) sawdust
Tea light

Method

Fill your smoker with the sawdust and level the top, then place it in your barbecue where the coals would normally go and light it using the tea light. On the grill where your food to be barbecued would go, place anything you want to cold smoke on a dish.

For smoked bacon butter, smoke the bacon, then cook until crispy, pat dry and cool. Grind to a fine powder and mix into softened unsalted butter.

For smoked chilli butter, smoke the chilli, finely chop and combine with softened unsalted butter. Or use chipotle peppers (dried smoked jalapeños).

For smoked garlic butter, smoke the garlic, then roast to concentrate the flavour. Use a stick blender to puree with a little oil, then fork into softened unsalted butter.

Smoky combinations

Chipotle butter – delicious on a spicy breakfast omelette.

Smoked bacon butter – melting over Brussels sprouts.

Smoked chilli butter – on jacket potatoes.

Smoked garlic butter – for an unusual garlic bread.

Smoked salt in butter – on new potatoes or a great addition to a cheeseboard.

Smoked unsalted butter – beautiful on mashed potatoes.

Spicy Butters

A really effective way to give an exotic twist to your dish and take it to India, Mexico, Africa or anywhere that has a rich history of spice.

Method

If using dried spices, toast the spices to release the aromatic oils. Cool, and if using whole spices, grind to a powder. Add 1 teaspoon to 75g softened unsalted butter and combine.

If using fresh spices such as chillies, chop finely, then use a fork to combine with softened unsalted butter. Same goes for jasmine flowers (fresh or dried).

Spicy combinations

Chilli butter – with steak or prawns, brushed on roti bread or stirred through basmati rice.

Cinnamon and mixed spice butter – spread thickly on Jamaican ginger cake.

Cracked black pepper butter – push under the skin of a chicken breast before cooking.

Cumin, coriander and chilli butter – gorgeous on chicken.

Fennel seed butter – best friends with grilled white fish.

Garlic, chive and Szechwan pepper butter – on flash-fried squid.

Jalapeño butter – on refried beans.

Jasmine butter – for sticky rice.

Moroccan spiced butter – brushed over hot flat breads.

Mustard powder and red onion (see Herby butters, page 62) butter – brushed over roast beef.

Pink peppercorn and caper butter – for fish.

Smoked paprika and nutmeg butter – on courgettes.

Sumac butter – stirred through jewelled couscous.

Sweet Butters

Flavoured sweet butters are everything you imagine and more; and when melting over a hot pudding or standing tall on a cupcake, they make your heart sing and will pick the dessert up and take it in a whole new direction.

Method

Beat 200g icing sugar (or soft brown sugar) into 100g softened unsalted butter. When completely combined, add the flavouring.

For the spices, toast them first to release the aromatic oils. Cool, and if using whole spices, grind to a powder. Add 1 teaspoon to 75g softened unsalted butter and combine.

For the coffee and chocolate, dissolve 1 teaspoon of instant coffee or cocoa powder in a tiny amount of hot water. Cool, and add to softened butter a little at a time while continually beating.

For the honey, add 3–4 teaspoons of runny honey to 100g softened unsalted butter and beat with a wooden spoon.

For the fudge, salted caramel and toffee butters, simply melt and leave to cool slightly before beating into softened butter.

Sweet combinations

Brown sugar and cinnamon butter – on cold Christmas pudding.

Cinnamon and raisin butter – with bread and butter pudding.

Coffee butter – on chocolate cake.

Chocolate and brown sugar butter – on cappuccino cake.

Chocolate butter – coffee and walnut cake.

Fudge butter – cupcakes.

Honey butter – a beautiful accompaniment to your buttermilk American-style pancakes (see page 39) and crispy bacon.

Salted caramel butter – on muffins.

Toffee butter – cupcakes.
Vanilla butter – cupcakes.

Wild Butters

Off the beaten track, quite literally, these butter flavours are as out there as it gets and they certainly have the wow factor, but much, much more than that, they add something special that nothing cultivated can match.

Method

For anything foraged, make doubly certain it is what you think it is. Wash it thoroughly in a sink full of salty water before using.

For the clover flowers, horseradish, juniper, truffle, wild garlic and wood sorrel, chop and add to softened unsalted butter.

For the puffball mushroom, slice thinly and dehydrate: place the slices – making sure they don't overlap – on a piece of kitchen paper and pop it on a radiator or next to the fire; after a day or two they should be dry. Alternatively, place the slices on a wire rack and leave in the oven when it's still warm after you've finished using it, and leave to dry in the residual heat. Blitz in a food processor or coffee grinder and stir into softened unsalted butter. And if your foraging trip is unsuccessful, try shop-bought dried mushrooms.

For the rose petals, place the petals on kitchen paper and put in an airing cupboard until dry. Tear up and knead gently into softened unsalted butter, leaving a few to sprinkle over the top.

For the samphire, if the leaves are young and tender, you can simply chop them finely before adding to softened unsalted butter; otherwise boil or steam them for 6–8 minutes before chopping.

For the stinging nettles, cook as spinach, squeeze all the moisture out and leave to one side to cool and dry out. Chop and add to softened unsalted butter.

Wild combinations

Clover flowers (*Trifolium*) butter – with red meat.
Dried puffball mushroom powder (*Calvatia gigantea*) butter – to finish off mushroom risotto.

Dried rose petals (*Rosa*) butter – melted as a dip for toasted pitta bread.

Fresh horseradish root (*Armoracia rusticana*) butter – melting on a rib-eye steak.

Juniper butter – on crackers with a glass of G&T.

Rock samphire (*Crithmum maritimum*) – sings like Pavarotti when served with scallops or any white fish.

Smoked salmon and fresh horseradish root (*Armoracia rusticana*) butter – on hot toast.

Stinging nettle (*Urtica dioica*) butter – with pasta or gnocchi.

Truffle (*Tuber*) butter – over scrambled eggs.

Wild garlic aka ramsons (*Allium ursinum*) butter – leaves in the late spring/early summer, bulbs in the winter – for a subtle, gentle garlic butter.

Wood sorrel (*Oxalis acetosella)* and brandy butter – for roast peaches and nectarines, or maybe to finish off Citrus pond pudding (see page 134).

COOKING IN BUTTER

If you're an experimental, creative cook who likes to get your elbows out in the kitchen and play with flavours, cooking in butter is going to bring joy to your heart. Anything cooked in butter automatically gets extra taste points. Butter adds depth and richness, succulence and flavour. And it's also an amazing vehicle to introduce other flavours, such as spices and herbs.

Spicy buttery rubs for your Sizzling Summer Signature Barbecue Dish will have neighbours and friends queuing around the block. But like everything to do with butter, there are tips and tricks to getting it right, and that's what we're going to look at here.

In this section we'll explore the four main ways of cooking in butter:

As a rub
Confit
Sauté
Sous vide

Each will add something exciting and different to your cooking, and if you're already freaking out thinking it looks complicated, remember I am currently living in a caravan (while building a house) and have a minute kitchen you couldn't swing a cat in, although that might have more to do with the fact that I also live with two Great Danes who would take particular exception to me bringing pussycats in full stop, let alone swinging them around the kitchen. But the point still stands, if I can do it here, anyone can do it anywhere.

Butter as a rub

There are arguments between aficionados over which are best, wet rubs or dry rubs. But as this is a book on butter, we're going to go wet buttery rubs all the way. Butter rubs are marinating with attitude. It's physical, messy and incredibly tactile, and is a brilliant way of getting succulence and heaps of flavour into your food.

So far, so good. But there is a problem with butter rubs that you need to be aware of. Butter has a low smoke point, meaning it cooks and browns fast. The upshot is that whatever you're cooking will look done on the outside long before the middle has had a chance to cook through. A good solution is to buy a meat thermometer and use it while the food is cooking to ensure it's cooked all the way through.

Equipment
Bowl
Meat thermometer

Ingredients
Good-quality unsalted butter
Herbs/spices
Fish, meat or vegetables

Method
Bring the butter up to room temperature. Add the herbs/spices and incorporate. Coat the meat, fish or vegetable as follows:

Fish Go gentle: yes these are rubs, but we don't want to end up with a mush and fish should always be treated delicately. If, like me, you're not a fan of skin you can remove it before adding the rub, but that's optional.

Meat We can afford to be a little more proactive here. Completely cover the meat and massage the rub in to really get the flavours absorbed. For best results do this the night before you want to cook and leave in the fridge.

Poultry The trick with this is to get the buttery rub underneath the skin, so first take your chicken, turkey, whatever, and gently ease your hands between the skin and the flesh to create a pocket under the skin. Now fill that pocket with your rub.

Vegetables Prepare the vegetables, then toss them in the buttery rub with your hands until they are all coated.

Now you've got the principles, it's time, ladies and gentlemen, for buttery Armageddon. Less is for wimps. We want more, more, more. More flavour, more heat, more everything. Roasted in the oven or cooked on the barbecue, here are my ten best-ever butter rub recipes.

Fiery hot roast beef rub

The butter will melt and give succulence while the spices will form an amazing crust of flavour that sings all over beef. You can use this with any cut of beef, but it goes particularly well with brisket, long slow roasted.

50g unsalted butter
1 teaspoon dark brown sugar
1 teaspoon lightly crushed mixed peppercorns
1 teaspoon mustard powder
1 teaspoon paprika
1 teaspoon chilli powder
1 teaspoon garlic powder
1 teaspoon ground cumin
1 teaspoon salt

1 Soften the butter and work all the ingredients together, then coat the beef, massaging it in. Cover and pop in the fridge for at least 2 hours. Take it out and bring up to room temperature before cooking.

Classic poultry rub

With this rub, poultry need never be dry and tasteless. The acid from the lemon and the creaminess of the butter work together to keep the bird moist, while the garlic and herbs infuse the meat with complementary flavours.

50g unsalted butter
Juice of 1 lemon
2 cloves garlic, chopped
1 teaspoon dried thyme
1 teaspoon lightly crushed pink peppercorns
½ teaspoon salt

1   Mix the butter and lemon juice, then add the garlic, thyme, peppercorns and salt and mix well. Gently push the rub under the skin of the bird.

Outback rib rub

This is influenced by some of the rubs in America, where flavouring pork ribs is a big thing. Not one for the faint-hearted, this is a two-step process starting with a marinade the day before you want to cook, then adding the rub just before cooking.

For the marinade
500ml of your favourite beer
2 tablespoons soft dark brown sugar
2 teaspoons salt
2 teaspoons ground cumin

For the rub
2 tablespoons unsalted butter
1 tablespoon vegetable oil
1 tablespoon balsamic vinegar
1 teaspoon runny honey
1 teaspoon lightly crushed mixed peppercorns
1 teaspoon white pepper
1 teaspoon cayenne pepper
1 teaspoon chilli powder
1 teaspoon garlic powder
1 teaspoon smoked paprika
1 teaspoon dried oregano
1 teaspoon salt

1   For the marinade, put the beer, sugar, salt and cumin in a saucepan and warm, stirring until the sugar has dissolved. Transfer to a bowl and set to one side to cool completely. When cold, lay the ribs flat in a shallow tray and pour over the marinade, cover and leave in the fridge for 24 hours.
2   For the rub, blend the butter, oil, vinegar and honey, then add all the dry ingredients and mix. Take the ribs out of the brine and pat dry with kitchen paper before coating with the rub.

Super smooth salmon rub

Because salmon has quite a delicate taste, it's all too easy to obliterate the flavour completely. The trick is to help the salmon shine, bring it out into the spotlight, and that's exactly what this rub does. This recipe is enough for two sides of salmon.

100g unsalted butter
1/2 teaspoon salt
1 tablespoon finely chopped chervil
1 tablespoon finely chopped dill
1/2 clove garlic, crushed
Twist of black pepper
Grated zest of 1 unwaxed lemon

1   Bring all the ingredients together, then rub half over one salmon side, then the other half over the second side. Sandwich the two sides, rubbed sides together, and wrap tightly in foil, then bake or barbecue.

Chocolate steak rub

Chocolate on steak is an unexpectedly good combination. The richness of the chocolate and the smoothness of the butter melting into the steak bring something utterly unique to this dish.

50g unsalted butter
1 teaspoon cocoa powder
1 teaspoon finely chopped fresh tarragon
½ teaspoon hot paprika
½ teaspoon coarsely ground peppercorns
½ teaspoon flaked sea salt

1   Mix all the ingredients together and coat the top side of a steak. Cover and leave in the fridge for at least 2 hours. Then barbecue, standing well back from the smoke and flames as the butter drips off the steak and onto the coals!

Anchovy lamb rub

Talk about bringing out the flavour – anchovies ramp up the lambiness like nothing else, while the butter melts and tenderises this slow roast shoulder joint.

100g unsalted butter
6 salted anchovy fillets
1 teaspoon finely chopped fresh sage
1 teaspoon finely chopped fresh rosemary
¼ teaspoon ground cumin
¼ teaspoon freshly ground black peppercorns

1   Mash the anchovies into the butter, then combine the sage, rosemary, cumin and peppercorns. Make slashes in the lamb shoulder and rub well in. Pop in a roasting bag, seal and bake.

Coffee-butter pork rub

The coffee butter picks up the flavour of the pork and hurls it into the stratosphere. Honestly, until you've tried a coffee-butter pork rub, you haven't lived. It works beautifully on a tenderloin or fillet seared in a pan and finished off in the oven.

50g unsalted butter
1 teaspoon finely ground fresh coffee
1 teaspoon finely chopped fresh sage
½ teaspoon sea salt
½ teaspoon ground white pepper

1   Mix all the ingredients together and slather over the pork. Cover and leave in the fridge for at least 2 hours. Bring up to room temperature before cooking.

Garden vegetable rub

This buttery rub will bring a wow to your vegetables. Perfect for a medley of sweet potato wedges, Brussels sprouts, cauliflower florets and asparagus spears.

50g unsalted butter
1 tablespoon finely chopped summer savory
2 tablespoons finely chopped wild garlic (ramsons) leaves or bulbs
1/2 teaspoon fine sea salt
1/2 teaspoon freshly ground black pepper

1   In a bowl mix the butter, summer savory, wild garlic, salt and pepper. Bring it all together and add your selection of raw vegetables. Toss with your hands until everything is covered. Tip into a baking tin and bake in the oven until the potato wedges are soft.

Incredibly buttery mushroom rub

This rub will transform mushrooms into a sexy, buttery plate of happiness. The trick is to take a teaspoon and scoop out the dark underside gills from the mushrooms before coating them with the rub: it's the gills that carry water and removing them gives the mushroom itself a more intense flavour. Couple that with this buttery rub and your eyes will ping when you try one.

50g unsalted butter
2 cloves garlic, crushed
1 tablespoon chopped fresh thyme
1 tablespoon freshly grated Parmesan cheese
¼ teaspoon finely ground black pepper

1   In a bowl combine the butter and garlic, then add the thyme, cheese and pepper and bring it all together. Add your raw mushrooms, prepared as above, and move them around carefully with your hands until all are coated, using any spare butter to spread thickly inside the mushrooms until no butter is left. Roast in the oven on high until cooked.

Barnstorming barbecue rub

A good all-purpose rub for your barbecue is worth its weight in
gold, and this is a barnstormer! Works well with any meat and
will give everything a buttery, spicy, va-va-voom.

100g unsalted butter
1 tablespoon hot smoked paprika
1 tablespoon sweet smoked paprika
4 cloves garlic, crushed
2 teaspoons Worcestershire sauce
1 teaspoon onion powder
1 teaspoon dried porcini salt

1   In a large bowl, bring all the ingredients together until
    completely mixed. Tumble in your uncooked sausages,
    chops, steaks, chicken drumsticks and whatever else is going
    on your barbecue and give them all a good massage. When
    you cook, stand well back as butter dripping onto hot coals
    will create smoke and flames.

TIP
If you can't buy porcini salt, you can use porcini powder.

Confit

Means to long slow cook in a bath of fat at a low temperature. Mmm mmm, doesn't that sound appetising? Granted, there are sexier sounding cooking methods, although if you've ever tasted anything that has been properly confit'ed there's not much sexier, because it's *stunning*! And it doesn't taste greasy, far from it!

Confit came about as a method of preserving meat and vegetables (and fruits, but they are confit'ed in a syrup and we're only concerned with butter here) in the years BF – Before Fridges – so in that respect it's in the same bracket as sausages, bacon and salami; at some point confit stopped being necessary for preserving, but it's still really stunning to eat.

The process begins by curing overnight in a strong brine (salt solution), followed the next day by that long slow cooking in fat at a low temperature. This part of the process is critical. Choose as small a saucepan as you can – just large enough for the food you want to confit – and fill it with just enough melted butter to submerge your meat or vegetables.

When it comes to the cooking, you don't want the butter to brown, go nutty and influence the taste, so it's imperative you keep the temperature below boiling point. Cook gently for 3–4 hours. The long slow heating begins breaking down the meat's connective tissue, so when you eat it it's soft and tender and melt in the mouth.

When it's done, while it's still hot, transfer the meat/vegetables into a heat-resistant jar and top up with the butter you cooked it in, right the way to the top. By doing this your produce will be out of the reach of bacteria, and so won't spoil anywhere near as quickly, and would happily last months in the fridge.

To reinvigorate your confit meat/vegetables, take them out, wipe away any excess butter, place them in a baking tin and cook quickly at high temperature until crispy. Serve and prepare to fall in love.

Confit meat

Select a meat that lends itself to tenderising, such as duck legs, chicken wings or pork belly strips, goose – or poultry offal such as gizzards (*gésiers* in French), hearts and testicles (yes really, cockerel testicles are a delicacy and taste like scallops). Remember to only use pieces of a size that will fit into your storage jar.

Equipment
Bowl
Small saucepan
Heat-resistant storage jar with lid

For the brine
4 litres water
500g fine sea salt
2 tablespoons sugar
Aromats (bay leaf, juniper berries, peppercorns)

For the confit
500g unsalted butter

1 Make up your brine in the bowl, stirring to ensure the salt and sugar are fully dissolved. Add the aromats, then submerge your meat in the brine and leave for at least 6 hours.
2 Remove the meat from the brine, rinse and pat dry. Warm the butter in a pan until it's melted, but not boiling. Add the brined meat and cook just under simmering point for 3–4 hours.
3 Place the meat in the jar while still hot, pour in the butter to cover the meat and seal with the lid.

VEGETABLES
Any root vegetable works beautifully – potatoes, carrots, parsnips, beetroot, etc. – as do vegetables with a high sugar content such as courgettes, garlic, and even small whole tomatoes.

Follow the method for confit meat, but adjust the cooking time down to 1 hour.

Sauté

Frying to you and me, but in a small amount of very hot butter. Predominantly used for vegetables such as potatoes, courgettes, aubergines or cauliflower, the hot butter caramelises the natural sugars in the vegetables, giving a crispy coating and smooth buttery finish.

When preparing root vegetables such as potatoes and carrots, the trick is to cut the vegetables into rounds, parboil them, drain, cover and leave to one side to cool. When you're ready to sauté, heat a small amount of butter in a shallow pan until sizzling. Carefully place a single layer of vegetables into the butter. Turn only once to prevent them breaking up. Both sides of the vegetables should be crisp and brown.

Sous vide

This is French for 'under vacuum': in practice it usually means cooking in a vacuum-sealed bag in a water bath at a controlled low temperature. Adding butter gives an extra special flavour. A steak cooked sous vide would leave it so buttery soft and tender you could cut it with a spoon, while still being exactly how you like it – rare, medium or spoilt.

That said, the equipment isn't cheap. You will need a vacuum packer and a sous vide machine, both of which will cost a pretty penny. The DIY version involves a bag squished of air and tied tight, a saucepan of water, a thermometer and a lot of patience.

Beef, venison, rabbit, pheasant, any firm, lean meat would work well. Take a steak along with 50g of unsalted butter and place them in a bag. Vacuum seal, and drop it into the water bath for 4–7 hours – or as much as 48 hours. Take the steak out of the bag and sear on both sides on a hot griddle to caramelise all those lovely buttery juices before serving.

BUTTER SAUCES

A sauce is to food what a killer pair of shoes are to an outfit: it will give it a boost if it's good or distract if it's bad. It's the touch of style and class that shows the world you know what you're doing – and it's no coincidence that the best butter sauces are French.

These buttery sauces should be a part of your cooking repertoire, as there is hardly a dish you can't pour a little flavour magic over to make it even more scrumptious and appealing, and your family and friends will love you for them.

The key points when making butter sauces are to use unsalted butter so you can control the seasoning, give yourself plenty of time and get the temperatures right.

Beurre blanc

Literally translated as 'white butter', this classic sauce is based on a reduction of shallots, vinegar and white wine; small pieces of chilled butter, and a spoonful of double cream, are gradually whisked in. It goes beautifully with fish.

Hollandaise

One of the five mother sauces in French cuisine, Hollandaise is an emulsion of melted butter, egg yolks and lemon juice, and should be satiny smooth. Delicious with eggs (eggs Benedict, eggs Florentine) and asparagus spears.

Béarnaise

If Hollandaise is a mother sauce, then Béarnaise is the only-just-a-little-less-important child. The difference is the flavouring, as the acid in Béarnaise comes from white wine vinegar rather than (in Hollandaise) lemon juice. It also includes finely chopped shallots and tarragon. Gorgeous with meat and fish.

Sauce velouté

Another of the five mother sauces, sauce velouté (from the French word for 'velvety') is made with stock and thickened with a roux of butter and flour. It is the 'mother' of many other classic sauces, such as sauce allemande (velouté thickened with egg yolk and double cream) or sauce supreme (velouté flavoured with mushrooms and cream), enjoyed with poultry, particularly chicken.

Beurre noisette

Also known as brown butter, this is a simple sauce of butter melted until the colour begins to darken. It's an ideal accompaniment to fish, especially flat fish, pasta and vegetables. **Meunière butter** is beurre noisette flavoured with a good squeeze of lemon juice.

Beurre manié

Not a sauce in itself, but a thickening agent for other sauces, beurre manié is made with equal parts flour and butter that you knead together to form a soft paste. Drop a little into a simmering stew at the very last minute and stir in to thicken. The butter will prevent the flour from lumping, while also giving a nice buttery note to your dish.

USING CLARIFIED BUTTER AS A SEALANT

The main reason food spoils is because bacteria get to it. The solution is to block the bacteria's progress. Simple. At least it would be if bacteria weren't such accomplished warmongers. But in this fight we do have weapons at our disposal, namely: fridges, freezers, salt, sealable containers and clarified butter.

Because the milk solids have been removed from clarified butter it doesn't go bad quickly, so when we use it as an airtight 'lid' over food stored in a jar or tub, it acts as a natural sealant that bacteria can't penetrate. There are two methods of using clarified butter in this way: potting and sealing.

Potting

Cooked meat or fish is added to melted clarified butter and then transferred to a pot or tub to cool. It is important that there is enough clarified butter to completely cover the meat or fish, as it's this barrier that will protect it from going off.

Typical potted dishes include...

- Potted shrimps
- Potted beef
- Potted crab
- Potted game
- Potted lobster

Sealing

This differs from potting in that the clarified butter isn't mixed in with the meat or fish, but poured over the top as a barrier. This method lends itself to pâtés and parfaits rather than chunks of meat or fish.

MAKING BUTTER ICING

Sweet buttery topping for cakes and cupcakes, loved by everybody, simple to make, gorgeous to eat, come on, who doesn't know what butter icing is? Beat butter and icing sugar together, end of story. Or is it?

No, of course not! Butter is an amazing vehicle for other flavours and colours, and using it for the topping on your favourite cakes is no different. Now you *can* go out and buy flavourings and colourings for butter icing, or you can make your own with natural ingredients. Adding vegetables to cakes has a long tradition, so don't be put off, and in the quantities used you can barely taste them. The trick is to have a light touch and add the colouring gradually so you can judge the effect. Always use unsalted butter, so you can control the flavour.

You'll need a juicer to make beetroot and carrot juice. For grape juice, remove any seeds from black grapes and then puree the grapes with their skins.

Cook spinach or nettles briefly until soft, then squeeze out all the moisture and puree. Slice red cabbage and boil in a little water; remove the cabbage, leaving the purple water; add a pinch of baking soda until the water turns blue.

Natural colourings for butter icing

- Beetroot juice for light pink to vivid red.
- Carrot juice for orange.
- Ground cinnamon with a little strong coffee for brown.
- Cocoa powder for very dark brown/black.
- Grape juice for purple.
- Red cabbage and baking soda for blue.
- Spinach/stinging nettles for green.
- Ground turmeric for yellow.

Natural flavourings for butter icing

When flavouring butter icing, always start with a small pinch of salt. I know it sounds counter-intuitive, but that sprinkling will really help bring out the added flavours.

- Banana
- Melted chocolate
- Coconut cream
- Jam
- Lemon juice and grated zest
- Grated orange zest
- Vanilla sugar

For more ideas, why not look at some of the flavoured butters starting on page 56?

BUTTER DRINKS

Since bulletproof coffee became a thing... Wait, you *have* heard of bulletproof coffee, right? Actually, it probably does deserve a quick recap.

Bulletproof coffee is a drink made from coffee beans with added butter and oil. It was invented by entrepreneur David

Asprey from Albuquerque, New Mexico. While trekking in Tibet, he tried the local yak butter tea and was astonished to find how good it made him feel. Back home he played with the recipe and came up with a breakfast drink he called bulletproof coffee, that is claimed to improve everything from mental capacity to weight loss.

Now, although many people swear by it, and by many people I mean people in the public eye, sportsmen and women, company directors and some leading industry hot-shots, and there *is* some science behind the claims, it's important to state that there are also sceptics. Basically, if the science interests you, I encourage you to do your own research.

However, what is beyond question is how the drink made America sit up and take notice, and how quickly butter in drinks became highly fashionable. Hot drinks, cold drinks, alcoholic and soft, together with some amazing cocktails, butter is now the trendy new kid on the block.

Of course those people in Tibet sipping their yak butter tea are looking over at America and wondering what all the fuss is about. So that's where we'll start, at the source.

Yak butter tea (*po cha*)

Made with tea, salt and butter, this highly calorific beverage is the traditional drink around the regions of the Himalayas, most famously Tibet. Several bowls will be drunk before work, which you imagine would give you all the energy you need to scale a peak or two.

As with many cultures, there is beautiful ceremony surrounding the tea. Visitors are always offered tea, and invited to sip from a wooden bowl that is topped up between every mouthful so the bowl never empties.

Traditionally, the tea is made over a day-long process of steeping the leaves, then churning the thick, treacle-like liquid with hunks of yak butter and salt. In the Himalayas it tastes amazing. In south-east London on a cold winter afternoon, it's an acquired taste. So this recipe is a slightly westernised version, ideal for our equivalent of climbing mountains – a rather vigorous step class.

SERVES 2

2 teaspoons loose leaf black tea
200ml full cream milk
2 tablespoons unsalted butter (yak if you have it; if not, cow's butter is fine)
¼ teaspoon salt
Sugar to taste

1   Make the tea in a teapot and leave to one side to steep for at least 10 minutes.
2   Meanwhile, put the milk, butter and salt in a small saucepan and bring up to a simmer, stirring all the while.
3   Remove the saucepan from the heat and, using a stick blender, whizz the mixture until soft and bubbly.
4   Pour half a cup of the strong tea. Add the milky butter to the tea all the way to the top, adding sugar to taste.

Butter coffee

Drunk first thing in the morning, this is going to zoom you into your day like nothing on earth (it's also a really good hangover cure). If you've not had it before, do go easy as that zoom effect can work its way down and upset your tummy and nobody wants that at the office.

More than three million people across America are said to start their day with butter coffee. They firmly believe their concentration levels increase, their thoughts are clearer and their metabolism boosted. So there must be something to it. Mustn't there?

The facts show, well, yes, kind of. Made with good-quality unsalted ghee, good-quality coffee and the best coconut oil, the first thing to mention is the quality of the ingredients, which helps. Then there are the good fats and vitamins in the butter and oil, along with the caffeine that naturally increases both heart rate and metabolism, the effect of which is a long-lasting gentle coffee high. However, at 400 calories a pop, it's best taken early in the morning before a work-out and not on a lazy Sunday.

For this recipe I've plumped for ghee from cows who have been well looked after and grass fed, as it's 'cleaner', less sickly and better for you, although there's no reason why you can't use any good unsalted butter instead. The only proviso is you can't use instant coffee. It doesn't work.

SERVES 1

1 cup of coffee made with freshly ground coffee beans
1 tablespoon high welfare grass fed unsalted ghee (or good-quality unsalted butter)
1 teaspoon coconut oil

1 Make the coffee as you like it in a beaker or high-sided container.
2 Add the ghee (or butter) and coconut oil. Using a stick blender, whizz until frothy.

Butterbeer

Break out your wizarding wand and cloak – this drink, inspired by the Harry Potter books and the infamous tipple served in The Three Broomsticks, is really rather good, and you can't help but be intrigued when Harry claims it's the most delicious thing he'd ever tasted.

The drink is creamy and sugary and served hot with whipped cream or ice cream floating on the top, and butterscotch sauce drizzled over that. Come on!

SERVES 4

300ml full cream milk
2 tablespoons unsalted butter
2½ tablespoons soft brown sugar
175ml cream soda
250ml double cream, whipped, or vanilla ice cream

For the butterscotch sauce
150ml single cream
150g soft dark brown sugar
50g salted butter
Vanilla essence
Tot of whisky (optional)

1 First make the butterscotch sauce: add all the ingredients to a saucepan and gently heat until thoroughly mixed.
2 Turn up the heat and stir constantly until the sauce has thickened, then remove from the heat. For the adult version, add the whisky. Put to one side for a couple of hours to cool.
3 In a saucepan heat the milk, butter and sugar, stirring constantly until completely combined and the milk is starting to foam up.
4 Take 2 tablespoons of the butterscotch sauce and mix it in. Then add the cream soda and immediately pour into a glass mug.
5 Top with whipped cream or ice cream, and drizzle with butterscotch sauce.

MAKE YOUR OWN BUTTER

20 buttery cocktails that will rock and roll your world

Cocktails were invented for people with imagination. People who understand that mixing flavours can spin you off into a taste sensation that will excite and amuse your palate in ways that nothing else can. And for hen parties.

Their names are familiar to us from the films that made them famous: Singapore Sling, Manhattan, Sidecar, White Russian. But it's hard to recall a beautiful leading lady on the big screen hopping up on a bar stall so the split in her skirt reveals her long sexy legs and asking, 'Can you add butter to mine?' And that's a shame, because cocktails with butter in are *amazing*!

Anything to do with mixology can be as complicated or as easy as you like. There are processes such as butter washing that will span a couple of days, but, trust me, it's worth it and the taste will blow your mind.

Cocktails are an experience designed to hit all five of your senses, and because of that everything's important, from the correct glass to the right ingredients, and of course the little accents on the side. A cocktail shaker with a built-in strainer is a very useful piece of kit.

If the recipe calls for rimming, it means putting a ring of caster sugar around the rim of the glass. This is done simply by turning the glass upside down and dipping the rim in water, and then in sugar. If a frozen glass is called for, run it under the tap and put it wet in the freezer for an hour.

The cocktails have been divided into four groups:

Butter-washed cocktails
Buttermilk cocktails
Hot butter cocktails
Non-alcoholic buttery cocktails

All drinks serve one unless otherwise stated.

Butter-washed cocktails

Butter washing is a way of taking the flavour of butter and adding it to a spirit, but without the butter fats that would leave an unpleasant buttery scum floating on the surface. Once the spirit has been washed in butter, it's beautifully clear and clean tasting with just a background note of rich, creamy butter.

This is achieved by mixing melted butter (brown butter for a nutty finish) and spirit. Vodka works well, as does white rum, but you can pretty much use anything. Go 10:1, ten parts spirit to one part butter. Put the spirit and the melted butter in a jar together and shake well, then let it stand for four or five hours so the flavours can infuse. You then put the whole thing in the freezer for at least a day so the fats in the butter solidify, but the alcohol doesn't. Take it out and strain it through some muslin. Job done: butter-washed alcohol.

Butter Daiquiri

A buttery twist on an old favourite. The butter really comes through in this drink and gives it a very smooth finish.

1 part fresh lime juice
2 teaspoons sugar
Ice
3 parts butter-washed rum

1 Drench a martini glass under the tap and put it in the freezer.
2 Stir the lime juice and sugar together until the sugar has dissolved.
3 Fill your cocktail shaker with ice cubes, add the butter-washed rum along with the lime and sugar mix, and shake for about half a minute. Strain into your iced glass.

Utterly dandy

This is a big bold cocktail that is very concerned about how it looks. Although the ingredients are few, the flavours carry a punch, and the butteriness comes through a treat.

2 parts butter-washed vodka
2 parts water
½ teaspoon caramel sauce
Ice
Squeeze of lemon
Wedge of mango

1 Add the butter-washed vodka, water and caramel sauce to an ice-filled cocktail shaker and stir. Add a squeeze of lemon and strain into a martini glass.
2 Serve with a wedge of mango on the side of the glass.

Caramel sauce
250g caster sugar
150ml double cream
50g unsalted butter

1 Put the sugar in a pan with 4 tablespoons of water and heat until the sugar has dissolved, then turn up the heat and bubble for 4–5 minutes s until caramel coloured.
2 Take off the heat and carefully stir in the cream and butter. Leave to cool, then store in a jar.

Buttered vodka spritzer

Who'd have thought buttered vodka could be so refreshing?

   Ice
   2 parts butter-washed vodka
   Soda water
   Slice of lemon

1 Drench a martini glass under the tap and put it in the freezer.
2 Fill a cocktail shaker with ice cubes and add the butter-washed vodka. Shake well.
3 Strain into the iced glass. Top up with soda water and serve with a slice of lemon.

Damned if I'll be lonely tonight

This stunning cocktail is all about friends: honey and berries love vodka. Served in a tall glass, it's a long drink, smooth and refreshing with a lovely buttery undertone.

Juice of 1 lemon
2 tablespoons sugar
6 parts soda water
Ice
2 parts butter-washed vodka

For the honeyberry syrup
2 teaspoons runny honey
Juice of ¼ lemon
1 thumbnail-sized piece of fresh ginger, sliced
200g blackberries

1 First make the honeyberry syrup: add the honey, lemon juice and ginger to a saucepan and heat until bubbles begin to appear.
2 Add the blackberries, stir and simmer until reduced by half. Remove from the heat, strain and cool.
3 For the cocktail, mix the lemon juice, sugar and soda water in a jug.
4 Fill a highball glass with ice, then add your butter-washed vodka. Pour on the lemon soda water almost to the top of the glass.
5 Spoon the honeyberry syrup over the top.

MAKE YOUR OWN BUTTER

Randy as a drake

This simple drink hits the buttery mark as it incorporates butter and butter-washed vodka.

   ½ teaspoon butter
   4 drops of Tabasco or chilli oil
   Caster sugar
   1 shot ice cold butter-washed vodka

1   Melt the butter and add the Tabasco or chilli oil.
2   Rim a cold martini glass in the butter chilli oil, then into caster sugar.
3   Carefully pour in the ice cold butter-washed vodka.

Long island buttery iced tea

A buttery version of this classic that has not one, but two butter-washed spirits.

   Ice
   1 part butter-washed vodka
   1 part butter-washed rum
   1 part gin
   1 part orange liqueur
   1 part freshly squeezed orange juice
   1 part freshly squeezed lemon juice
   1 teaspoon sugar syrup
   1 can of cola

1   Fill a cocktail shaker with ice and add everything except the cola, and shake.
2   Pour into a highball glass and top up with cola.

Buttermilk/butter cocktails

Based around buttermilk, which is fat-free and really good for you, or good-quality (hopefully homemade) butter which has so many health benefits, these cocktails not only taste amazing but will make you feel great too. The buttery taste makes the cocktail rich and deep with a nice mouth-feel and a soft, creamy aftertaste.

Soft night

This brandy-based delight is totally indulgent and works beautifully with buttermilk.

> Ice
> 1 part buttermilk
> 2 parts aged brandy
> 1 part crème de cacao
> Grating of nutmeg to garnish

1 Fill your cocktail shaker with ice, add the buttermilk, brandy and crème de cacao and shake.
2 Pour out into a martini glass and garnish with a grating of nutmeg.

Summer afternoon

This is perfect for a hot, sticky summer's day when you want something deep and rich and tropical that makes you feel deliciously lazy in a hammock with a good book.

  1 part coconut liqueur
  2 parts vodka
  3 parts buttermilk
  4 parts pineapple juice

1 Add everything to an ice-filled cocktail shaker. Shake, then pour out into a tall glass.

Lounge lizard

This is a dark drink for dark nights, with butter, cream, rum and coffee.

  Dark roast coffee
  2 teaspoons unsalted butter
  2 parts rum
  1 part double cream
  Squeeze of lemon

1 Make a mug of strong black coffee.
2 Put the butter and rum into a heatproof glass. Pour on the coffee and give the butter time to melt.
3 Slowly pour in the cream so it floats, and finish with a squeeze of lemon.

All night blue

Sometimes a shot is the only thing that'll cut it. Vodka based with great colour and amazing taste.

  Ice
  1 part buttermilk
  1 part vodka
  1 part blue curaçao

1 Fill a cocktail shaker with ice. Add the buttermilk, vodka and blue curaçao, and shake for 30 seconds. Pour into a shot glass.

Hot butter cocktails

This is ramping up the flavour to the next level. Butter melting on toast or a jacket potato automatically wins prizes for the way it looks, smells and tastes. Now take that melting butter and add it to a liqueur or two and the whole world sits up a little straighter and starts smiling.

Homemade butter is best, otherwise good-quality butter is fine. Use it at room temperature rather than straight out of the fridge, and when the recipe calls for hot water to be poured over the top, give the butter time to melt before moving on to the next step. As these cocktails are hot, it is vitally important you use glasses appropriate for hot drinks.

Hot buttered rum

Deep and rich with a hint of the Caribbean. The honey dances with the rum while the butter gives it a soft, creamy finish.

> 1 teaspoon salted butter
> 1 teaspoon runny honey
> 2 parts Jamaican rum
> 4 parts hot water
> Pinch of ground cinnamon

1   Add the butter, honey and rum to a glass. Top up with hot water and stir until mixed. Sprinkle the cinnamon from a height so some of it gets caught on the glass rim.

Hot buttery comfort

This is an alcoholic hug that will make you feel warm and cosy. Surprisingly complex, the butter mellows the Southern Comfort while the heat intensifies the smell, which adds to the soothing sensation.

> 1 teaspoon unsalted butter
> 2 parts Southern Comfort
> 4 parts hot water
> Slice of peeled fresh ginger

1   Put the butter and Southern Comfort in a glass and top up with hot water. Drop in the fresh ginger, stir and serve.

Hot tot butter whiskey

A real winter warmer that will heat you from the inside out. Quite a clean, tight finish and definitely one for a cold winter's night.

2 teaspoons unsalted butter
¼ teaspoon caster sugar
6 parts hot water
2 parts whiskey
Pinch of ground cinnamon

1 Put the butter, sugar and hot water into a glass and stir until all the sugar has dissolved.
2 Pour on the whiskey and finish with a flourish of cinnamon.

Hot apple pie zinger

It will make you laugh, it will make you shake your head, and it will make you laugh some more. This is a hot apple pie in a cocktail glass.

1 teaspoon salted butter
½ teaspoon caster sugar, plus a little for rimming the glass
100ml hot water
Pinch of ground cinnamon
2 parts rum
1 clove
1 green apple

1   Place the butter and sugar in a jug and top up with hot water. Stir until all the sugar has dissolved.
2   Mix a little caster sugar and cinnamon together and use it to rim a glass.
3   Add the rum and the clove to the glass and pour on the butter, sugar and hot water mix.
4   Cut a neat wedge from an apple – do this last minute or the flesh will go brown – and pop it in the cocktail.

Hot buttery dessert wine

Serve this with pudding, especially anything fruity or citrus, and your kudos will go through the roof.

1 teaspoon salted butter
1 teaspoon maple syrup
2 parts hot water
4 parts dessert wine

1   Put the butter and syrup in a glass and add the hot water, stirring until completely combined.
2   Add the wine, stir and serve.

Non-alcoholic buttery cocktails

Up to now, we've been looking at ways to complement butter and spirits, which are natural best buddies to start with. But take away the spirits and suddenly it's a whole new challenge. The answer is not to make a regular buttery cocktail and omit the booze, any more than you'd serve a vegetarian a steak dinner, minus the steak. The gap is too big and glaring. No, we've got to re-invent it. Start again. Look at tastes and flavours and textures, how they come together to feel in your mouth, and the aftertastes. Luckily, butter is very versatile.

Butter apple juice

This is sure to be a massive hit with kids and adults alike. The
buttery apple gives it a really gorgeous aftertaste.

SERVES 2

500ml apple juice
2 tablespoons unsalted butter
1 tablespoon soft dark brown sugar
¼ teaspoon ground cinnamon
3 cloves
Grating of nutmeg
Pinch of salt
Basil leaves to garnish

1   In a pan over a medium heat, bring the apple juice to a
    simmer.
2   Add the butter and brown sugar and stir. Add the cinnamon,
    cloves, nutmeg and salt, stir and keep just below a simmer
    for about 10 minutes until all the flavours have infused.
3   Pour into heatproof glasses, top with a few basil leaves and
    serve.

Hot chocolate overload

Heaven has arrived in a glass! The addition of the buttermilk gives it a creamy, chocolaty taste you will love.

150ml buttermilk
2 teaspoons chocolate hazelnut spread
1 teaspoon vanilla sugar
Quenelle of chocolate ice cream
1 cinnamon stick to serve

1   Heat the buttermilk in a pan and briskly stir in the chocolate hazelnut spread and sugar. Pour into a glass.
2   Carefully float the ice cream quenelle on top. Serve with a cinnamon stick.

Refreshing buttery iced tea

The addition of butter gives iced tea an extra layer of creamy smoothness.

SERVES 4

4 mugs of boiling water
4 Earl Grey teabags
2 tablespoons unsalted butter
1 tablespoon runny honey
Ice
4 slices of lemon
4–6 slices of cucumber
2 vanilla pods
Sprig of mint

1 Make a medium-strong tea in a small saucepan then discard the teabags. While the liquid is still boiling hot, add the butter and honey, and leave it for a couple of hours to cool.
2 When it's thoroughly cold, the butter fats will have formed a crust on the top of the tea. Carefully, using a spoon, remove the crust.
3 Fill a jug with ice and pour in the tea. Add the lemon, cucumber, vanilla and mint, and serve.

Buttery banana daiquiri

If bananas and buttermilk were on Facebook their status would be in a relationship with each other. They were born to be together, and when used in a daiquiri they become their best selves.

1 large banana
250ml buttermilk
Juice of ½ a lime
30g caster sugar
Ice
Thin slice of lime

1   Into a blender put the banana, buttermilk, lime juice, sugar and ice. Blitz until smooth and frothy. Serve with a slice of lime twisted on the rim of a martini glass.

Cranberry and butter smash

Refreshing and gorgeous, the butter smoothes out the high notes of the other flavours, leaving it delightfully soft and thirst-quenching.

200ml cranberry juice
50ml pineapple juice
2 tablespoons unsalted butter, softened
1 teaspoon soft brown sugar
1/2 teaspoon allspice
1/2 teaspoon ground cinnamon
Grating of nutmeg
Pinch of salt
1–2 cloves

1   Into a jug add the cranberry, pineapple, butter, sugar, allspice, cinnamon, nutmeg and a pinch of salt. Using a stick blender, blitz until smooth and frothy.
2   Transfer into a tall glass with one or two cloves, and serve.

USING BUTTER AS A BEAUTY PRODUCT

Everyone wants to look and feel beautiful, it's part of being human. To achieve this we use what's around us. Now that might be the latest cream, ointment or lotion from the best beauty salon in town, but what if there isn't a beauty salon to go to? What if there are no shops at all? What if you live in ancient Egypt and your name is Cleopatra? You are celebrated as the most beautiful woman ever to have walked the earth, and will continue to be thought so for thousands of years to come. Yet with resources so scarce, how exactly did she achieve that? What was Cleopatra's beauty regime? Like us, she used what was around her, and milk and butter were a big part of that.

In this section, we're going to explore butter as a beauty product, and see if we can't tap into a little of that Egyptian beauty knowhow. Rich in protein, omega-3 and omega-6, a host of vitamins and beta carotene, for centuries butter was an essential product in natural beauty care. So let's take that a few steps further, and put together some beauty recipes that make sense today.

Today we swear by natural products such as avocados, coconuts and cucumbers for our beauty care, so it's really not that big a leap to include butter. However, as with all products, natural or not, always test a tiny amount first before you go full-on buttery facemask, especially if you have dairy allergies or intolerances. Take care to find the recipe that most suits your skin or hair type.

Buttery facemasks

Anyone who hasn't tried a facemask and felt that tingle as your skin rejuvenates hasn't lived. Whatever your skin concerns, be it complexion, hydration, tightening, toning, oily or dull skin, butter facemasks are an inexpensive, simple way to give your skin a natural boost.

However, as good and nutritious as butter is, it's not the full story as it would be way too greasy to use alone. So we mix it with other natural ingredients, each one designed to tackle a different concern. If you think about it, your skin is highly complex and individual, therefore the solution should mirror that. The trick, at least partly, is to search for a facemask that identifies your particular need. You can actually use more than one facemask at a time by layering them, and this will help if you feel you have several issues, although never go more than two or three, and never do the multi-pack more than once a week.

Preparation is key

Remove all makeup and exfoliate to open any blocked pores. Use a soft damp cloth or brush to apply the mask so there's no chance of bacteria transferring from your hands to your face. Set a timer so you don't leave the mask on for too long. Remove the mask by rinsing with warm water, then close the pores by splashing with cold water. Finally, moisturise to lock in all that goodness.

Do not leave the mask on too long. And as tempting as it is, using a facemask should not form part of your daily care regime as your skin needs time to relax between treatments.

Ingredients

2 tablespoons of the very best **unsalted butter** you can source. Homemade is infinitely better, but if you need to buy it, make certain you get butter from grass-fed, outdoor-raised cows with high welfare.

Add one or two of the following:

- 1 **strawberry** – naturally high in alpha hydroxy acids, known to help smooth fine lines and surface wrinkles. It is also rich in salicylic acid, a treatment for acne.
- The flesh from half an **avocado** – rich in natural oils, fats, vitamins, proteins and essential fatty acids, avocados are a great all-rounder to pep-up tired-looking skin.
- 1 tablespoon **lemon juice** – a natural astringent to clean and purify oily skin.
- 1 **egg yolk** – for dry skin.
- 1 tablespoon **Greek yoghurt** – thick and creamy moisturiser.

- Half a ripe **mango** – high in vitamin A, for keeping the skin firm and healthy.
- 2cm section of **cucumber** – to combat dark circles under the eyes.
- Half a soft mashed **banana** – for a natural moisturiser.
- 1 tablespoon **rose water** – for sun and wind-dried skin.
- 1 tablespoon **olive oil** – for an instant glow.
- 1 tablespoon **milk** – good treatment for oily skin.
- 1 tablespoon **coconut oil** – intense moisturising treatment.
- Juice from a **carrot** – for a healthy complexion.
- 2 tablespoons **salt** – helps remove dead skin.
- 2 tablespoons **peanut butter** – great for removing dirt and impurities while at the same time moisturising (but if you have an allergy to peanuts, avoid this treatment).

Method

In a bowl, add the butter and one or two ingredients from the list above. Mix and apply to face and neck. Leave the mask on for 10–15 minutes, then rinse thoroughly.

Buttery body mask

Treat your entire body to a mask for soft, beautiful skin. Simply multiply up the ingredients to make the desired amount, mix and apply all over. Leave for 10–15 minutes before rinsing.

Buttery hand treatment

Your hands bear the brunt of everything life has to throw at them, and can often become rough and dry. Decide how your hands feel and treat them to an appropriate hand mask. Mix the ingredients and apply all over your hands, massaging down between the fingers. Leave for 10–15 minutes before rinsing.

Buttery treatment for damaged hair

Hair can become damaged in any number of ways, resulting in it looking dry and lifeless without any shine or bounce. For a simple, natural buttery solution, melt 100g good-quality unsalted butter, and add to it 1 tablespoon coconut oil and 1 tablespoon natural yoghurt. Mix and comb into the hair, starting at the scalp and drawing it out to the ends until all the hair is completely covered. Put a shower cap over the top and leave for 20–30 minutes. Shampoo out and condition as normal.

13 SURPRISING USES FOR BUTTER

Of course there are other uses for butter. Mankind's ingenuity coupled with ten thousand years of butter making means we've learned a thing or two along the way. As we now know you can use butter in your hair, or on your face or body. You can drink it, eat it, cook with it. You can flavour it, culture it, shape it, wash it and even sculpt with it. But there's always more to the butter story.

These buttery tips and tricks are worth having in your 'Things to do in a crisis' repertoire.

Don't cut dry
Problems cutting packaging or tough plastic? If your knife or scissors simply won't cut it because they keep snagging, smear a little butter over the cutting surfaces and your sticky problem will be a thing of the past.

Gluey residue remover
Stickers, price labels, jam jar labels, it doesn't matter what you do, if you peel them off there's always an ugly residue. With a cloth and a little peanut butter, simply wipe the stain away.

This also works for anything gluey: children with glue on their hands after a craft session? Sap on your hands after picking up a stick for the dog or some over-enthusiastic tree hugging? Peanut butter is your answer.

Keep cheese fresh

Your cheese board went down a treat, but there's a load of cheese left over. Chances are, even if you cover it, the cut edges of the cheese will go hard and look unappealing. However, if you coat the cut edges in a thin layer of butter it will keep fresher for longer. This is a great tip if for any reason your cheese board is going to be out for any length of time before it's going to be used, like a buffet.

The 'butter on the cut surface' trick also works for halved onions.

Leather cleaner

Butter is a brilliant leather cleaner, from belts to wallets, purses to handbags. Put a little on a cloth and wipe the leather clean. Always test/try a little on a small patch first.

Also good for horse tack, though probably not the saddle as you might slip off.

Metal cleaner

Again, butter is a brilliant cleaner. Put a little on a cotton pad and rub to a shine. To remove deep tarnishing, mix the butter with a little lemon juice.

Peanut butter shaving cream

It's an emergency. You're out of shaving cream and there's no time to go out and buy some. Have you got some smooth peanut butter in the cupboard? Then no problem! The natural oils from the peanuts mean the razor will glide over your face or legs without nicking them and moisturise at the same time.

Ring removal

There is nothing in the world more annoying than standing in a jewellery shop having just tried on a ring with a diamond the size of the Ritz, and now you can't get it off your finger. A smear of butter and it should come sliding off.

Smells fishy

Preparing fish can leave your hands smelling like a trawlerman's coat. Soap and water alone won't shift it, but if you wipe your hands all over with butter first, and then wash with soap and water, the smell will go and your hands will be fresh and clean again.

Stop jam frothing

Add a teaspoon of butter to your fruit and sugar when making jam to stop it frothing.

Stop pasta boiling over

Pasta for dinner is supposed to be a quick solution, but if the pan boils over the clean-down can take longer than making the dish itself. If you add a tablespoon of butter to your boiling pasta water it will prevent it boiling over.

Swallowing medicine

Some of the tablets dispensed by pharmacists are so enormous you wonder if they didn't misunderstand what type of tablet you were asking for: 'Do you want me to swallow it or do a status update on it?' But fear not! Take it with a little butter and it slides down. If the taste is bad, try it with peanut butter.

WD-40 substitute

There's a squeak. It's driving you mad, and now the dog won't settle and every time someone opens the door he sits up and barks. What you need is some WD-40. What you have when you go searching in the shed is an empty can. Take a little butter and spread it on the squeak to cut it out.

Wild bird feeder

Calling all Scouts and Guides – remember getting a pine cone, rolling it in butter and then in birdseed before hanging it up for birds to come and feed from? Yeah, that.

CHAPTER 4

Recipes with butter as the headline act

Having explored just about everything you can do with butter, from making it to drinking it or conditioning your hair with it, it's time to step back and give it centre stage in 12 recipes that demonstrate just what a star ingredient it really is.

All the recipes are fully explained and easy to follow, and list all the equipment you'll need. The aim is to prepare a dish that when anyone tastes it, they'll look at you with a beaming smile and say, 'Ooh yeah, butter!' And what higher compliment is there?

Chicken liver parfait

A silky smooth butter-based pâté, best served spread on hot brown toast or Dutch-style crisp breads (crisp bakes) with a few green leaves and a handful of cherry tomatoes on the side.

SERVES 4

Equipment
Sharp knife
Small mixing bowl
Shallow wide pan
Blender or food processor
Fine sieve
Serving bowl or ramekins

350g chicken livers, trimmed (or try mixed poultry livers: if you cook a duck, goose or turkey with giblets, save the livers in the freezer until you have enough to make the parfait)
200ml full cream milk
1 large banana shallot, finely chopped
1 clove garlic, chopped
1 teaspoon olive oil
4 sprigs of fresh thyme
2 tablespoons brandy or dry sherry
250g butter, softened
Salt and freshly ground black pepper
Grating of nutmeg
50g clarified butter, melted

1 Place the chicken livers in the milk in a small bowl and leave to soak for half an hour. Drain on kitchen paper and pat dry.

2 In a shallow pan, gently fry the shallot and garlic in the olive oil until soft, then tip into a blender.

3 Add the livers to the pan and cook for a couple of minutes on each side, throwing in the thyme halfway through, until lightly coloured but still slightly pink in the middle – if you overcook them they will become grainy.

4 Pour in the brandy or sherry and simmer for a minute or two – you can flame the brandy if you like – then tip the livers into the blender with the cooked shallot and garlic. Blitz until you have a smooth puree.

5 Add the softened butter and blitz until combined, then add seasoning and nutmeg.

6 Press the mix through a fine sieve then transfer to a serving bowl or individual ramekins. Gently spoon over the clarified butter to cover completely, then place in the fridge.

7 Ready to eat after an hour but leaving the parfait to mature for a couple of days will help develop the flavours. Will keep for up to ten days if you don't break the butter seal.

Devilled fish

Griddled whole mackerel slathered in a fiery butter sauce, perfect with a crisp green salad and an ice cold glass of white wine.

SERVES 4

Equipment
Mixing bowl
Wooden spoon
Sharp knife
Griddle or barbecue

100g unsalted butter, softened
1 teaspoon each of:

- Fine sea salt
- English mustard powder
- Paprika
- Cayenne pepper
- Ground black pepper
- Ground coriander
- Ground cumin

2 teaspoons soft brown sugar
1 tablespoon white wine or cider vinegar
4 mackerel (or 8 sardines or herring)

1 Place the softened butter in a bowl and beat until light and fluffy. Add all the dry ingredients, including the sugar, and mix thoroughly.

2 Add the vinegar a few drops at a time and mix well between each addition to incorporate.

3 Using a sharp knife, slash the fish to the bone four or five times horizontally on each side.

4 Divide the butter between the fish and rub well into the slashes and into the body cavity.

5 Heat your griddle or barbecue until it is very hot. Grill the fish evenly on each side until cooked and the flesh flakes away from the bone easily. Serve hot.

Monkfish with smoked salmon butter

Succulent monkfish tail wrapped in smoky ham with luscious smoked salmon butter melting all over it. Delicious served with samphire and roasted cherry tomatoes.

SERVES 4

Equipment
Sharp knife
Food processor
Spatula
Clingfilm
Cocktail sticks
Ovenproof frying pan

75g unsalted butter, plus extra for frying
100g pack of smoked salmon trimmings or sliced smoked salmon
½ teaspoon fine sea salt
½ teaspoon coarsely ground pink peppercorns
Juice of 1 lemon
1 tablespoon finely chopped fresh flat-leaf parsley
1 large monkfish tail (or 4 small ones)
8 slices of dry-cured smoked streaky bacon, pancetta or smoked ham

1 Place the butter, smoked salmon, salt and pepper and lemon juice in a food processor and blitz until smooth. Remove the processor blade and stir in the chopped parsley.

2 Turn the butter onto a piece of clingfilm and form into a long, thin cylinder of 1.5cm diameter, wrap tightly and pop in the freezer for at least an hour.

3 Preheat the oven to 180°C/gas mark 4.

4 Carefully remove the bone from the monkfish, creating a pocket the length of the fish. Place the frozen butter into the pocket, trimming the length of the butter if necessary.

5 Lay out the slices of bacon/pancetta/ham side by side, overlapping slightly. Place your stuffed monkfish on top and wrap the monkfish in the bacon, securing with cocktail sticks.

6 Heat your ovenproof frying pan on the hob and pop in a small knob of butter to melt. When hot, place the monkfish in the pan and sear for 2 minutes on each side.

7 Place the pan in the oven for 25 minutes until the fish is just cooked through. Serve hot.

Chicken with garlic butter wrapped in Parma ham

Basted from the inside, this chicken breast stuffed with a garlic and herb butter is melt-in-the-mouth gorgeous. Serve with minted new potatoes and asparagus spears.

SERVES 4

Equipment
Sharp knife
Small mixing bowl
Spatula
Clingfilm
Meat mallet or rolling pin
Ovenproof frying pan
Meat thermometer

75g unsalted butter, plus extra for frying
2 cloves garlic, crushed
1 tablespoon finely chopped fresh lemon thyme
1 tablespoon finely grated Parmesan cheese
4 boneless skinless chicken breasts
8 slices of air-dried Parma or Serrano ham

1   In a bowl, mix together the butter, garlic, thyme and
    Parmesan to form a paste. Turn onto a piece of clingfilm and
    form into a long, thin cylinder of 1.5cm diameter, wrap
    tightly and pop in the freezer for at least an hour.

2   Remove the mini fillet from the underside of each chicken
    breast and place between two sheets of clingfilm. Using the
    mallet or rolling pin, gently hammer flat to a thickness of 2–
    3mm.

3   In the underside of each chicken breast, cut a pocket along
    two thirds of its length.

4   Unwrap the frozen butter cylinder and, using a knife that has
    been warmed under a hot running tap, cut it into four
    portions. Place a cylinder of the frozen butter into the pocket
    you have created in each chicken breast and place one of the
    flattened mini fillets over the top to seal it in.

5   Place two slices of ham, overlapping slightly, side by side on
    your work surface. Place one of the chicken breasts at a
    slight angle on top of the ham and wrap around, turning so
    the seam is on the underside. Repeat for the other three
    chicken breasts.

6   Preheat the oven to 180°C/gas mark 4.

7   Heat your ovenproof frying pan on the hob and pop in a small
    knob of butter to melt. When hot, place each chicken breast
    seam-side down in the pan and sear for 2 minutes. Turn and
    sear the second side for 2 minutes, then turn once more for
    another minute.

8   Place the pan in the oven for 25 minutes until the chicken is
    cooked through. To check the chicken is properly cooked,
    insert a meat thermometer into the fattest part of the
    chicken at an angle – you don't want to be testing the heat of
    the butter!

Butter chicken

A rich, luxurious curry. Serve with basmati rice and naan bread.

SERVES 4-6

Equipment
Sharp knife
Large bowl
Grater
Large heavy-based pan
Saucepan
Sieve

125g set natural yoghurt
Juice of 1 lemon
½ teaspoon ground cinnamon
½ teaspoon ground cardamom
½ teaspoon ground turmeric
½ teaspoon garam masala
1 teaspoon chilli powder
½ teaspoon ground white pepper
1kg chicken breasts, cut into strips
2 tablespoons vegetable oil
4 cloves garlic, crushed
2-3cm cube of fresh ginger, finely grated
2 tablespoons tomato puree
225g unsalted butter
400g tin chopped tomatoes
5cm piece of cinnamon stick, broken up
150ml single cream
2 red chillies, roughly chopped

1 In a bowl combine the yoghurt, lemon juice and spices. Add the chicken and mix well. Cover the bowl and leave in the fridge for at least 2 hours, or preferably overnight.

2 When you are ready to cook the curry, heat a large heavy-based pan on a medium heat, add the vegetable oil, garlic and ginger and fry for 1 minute while stirring.

3 Add the chicken and its marinade and stir-fry for 5 minutes.

4 Add the tomato puree and the butter and cook on a low heat for 10 minutes. Remove from the heat and set aside.

5 Put the chopped tomatoes and cinnamon into a saucepan, bring to the boil and simmer until the mixture has reduced by half. Press the tomato mix through a sieve into the chicken mix and discard the cinnamon.

6 Return the chicken mix to the heat, bring to the boil and simmer on a low heat for 5 minutes.

7 Add the cream, mix well and simmer for a further 5 minutes. Serve garnished with chopped chillies.

French peas and Little Gem lettuce

In this variation on a simple French classic, lettuce and peas are briefly braised together. Ideal accompaniment to grilled fish or meat.

SERVES 4

Equipment
Small bowl
Sharp knife
Saucepan with lid

75g unsalted butter, softened
50g plain flour
6 spring onions
2 Little Gem lettuce
500g frozen or fresh peas or petits pois
200ml vegetable stock
Salt and freshly ground black pepper

1   In a small bowl combine 50g of the butter with the flour,
    kneading with your fingertips to form a paste. Set aside in
    the fridge.
2   Peel the spring onions and cut into slices about 5mm thick,
    at an angle. Cut each lettuce in half lengthways, then cut
    each half into three, keeping the root attached.
3   Melt the remaining butter in a pan and sauté the sliced
    spring onions for 5 minutes.
4   Add the lettuce and sauté for a further 5 minutes, coating in
    the buttery juices.
5   Add the peas, stock and seasoning and stir gently. Bring to
    the boil, cover and simmer for 7 minutes.
6   Turn up the heat and add morsels of the butter/flour mix,
    stirring gently to incorporate and bringing the mixture to the
    boil between each addition – the butter mix will thicken the
    sauce. Serve immediately.

TIP
You may not need all the butter/flour mix; any leftover can be
kept in the fridge or freezer for future use.

Citrus pond pudding

Incredibly decadent, this steamed pudding oozes a pool of buttery, lemony syrup from a middle that hides a whole fruit. Serve with clotted cream, ice cream or custard.

SERVES 6

Equipment
1 litre pudding basin
Sieve
Mixing bowl
Palette (round-bladed) knife
Rolling pin
Fork
Large skewer
Greaseproof paper
Foil
String
Steamer or large pan

250g self-raising flour, plus extra for rolling
Pinch of salt
70ml milk
70ml water
120g shredded suet (beef or vegetable)
50g mixed dried fruit
120g unsalted butter, softened, plus extra for greasing
120g demerara sugar
1 unwaxed lemon

1   Grease the pudding basin. Sift the flour into a bowl and add the salt. Mix the milk and water together.

2   Add the suet and mixed fruit to the flour, then slowly add the milk and water and bring to a dough, using a palette knife – you may not need all the liquid, so add it gradually as you don't want a sticky dough. Turn out the dough and form into a ball.

3   Roll out the dough to about 6–8mm thick, in a roughly circular shape. Cut a quarter out of the dough, and form this into a small ball. Set aside.

4   Line the basin with the three-quarter portion of dough, bringing the edges together and sealing them using a little of the milk and water mix.

5   Using a fork, mix the butter and sugar together until combined, then put half the butter and sugar mix in the lined basin.

6   Prick the lemon all over using a large skewer, then put it in the basin. Cover the lemon with the rest of the butter and sugar mix. Brush the rim of the dough with water. Roll out the reserved dough to make a lid and press on top of the basin, sealing all round.

7   Take a square of greaseproof paper and place a square of foil on top (they should be big enough to cover the top of the basin and hang past the rim); make a pleat in the middle of the two together. Cover the dish tightly and tie it down with string.

8   Steam the pudding for about 4 hours – either in a steamer or in a large pan of water (water should come two-thirds of the way up the side of the basin) with an upturned saucer in the bottom. Keep checking to ensure the pan doesn't burn dry.

9   When cooked, remove the cover and turn the pudding out onto a plate with enough of a rim to collect all the butter lemon sauce that flows out. Serve hot.

Herb butter-roasted shallots

Sweet shallots in a herby butter sauce, to serve as a side with grilled fish or meat.

SERVES 4

Equipment
Sharp knife
Roasting tin suitable for hob
Large spoon

900g small shallots
75g unsalted butter
50ml olive oil
1 tablespoon chopped fresh thyme
1 teaspoon chopped fresh rosemary
1 teaspoon chopped fresh sage
Salt and freshly ground black pepper

1 Preheat the oven to 200°C/gas mark 6.
2 Remove the outer skins of the shallots but leave them whole with the roots still attached so they don't fall apart during cooking.
3 Melt the butter and oil in a roasting tin on the hob, add the shallots and lightly sauté for around 5 minutes or until evenly coated in the butter.
4 Add the chopped herbs and seasoning, toss all together and transfer to the oven to roast for around 40 minutes, basting frequently, until tender.

Stuffed stone fruit

Perfectly ripe peaches and nectarines, stuffed with an almond butter crumb and baked to perfection. Serve with clotted cream or ice cream.

SERVES 4

Equipment
Knife
Teaspoon
Mixing bowl
Large ovenproof dish or roasting tin

2 peaches
2 nectarines
2 yellow plums
50g Amaretti biscuits, crushed
2 tablespoons soft brown sugar
1 tablespoon ground almonds
1 tablespoon pistachio nuts, ground
1–2 tablespoons almond liqueur
40g unsalted butter, cut into 12 pieces
50ml dessert wine

1 Preheat the oven to 200°C/gas mark 6.
2 Halve and stone the fruit, then using a teaspoon scoop out some of the flesh from each half.
3 Chop the scooped-out flesh and place in a bowl. Add the crushed biscuits, sugar, nuts and enough almond liqueur to form a thick paste.
4 Stuff each fruit half with the biscuit mix and place in an ovenproof dish. Top each fruit half with a piece of butter, pour the dessert wine into the dish and bake for 40 minutes. Serve warm.

Chocolate brioche bread and butter pudding

Buttery brioche and three-fruit marmalade lift this classic pudding to a new and exciting level of indulgence.

SERVES 6

Equipment
Ovenproof dish
Bread knife
Butter knife
Saucepan
Mixing bowl
Whisk
Wooden spoon

675g chocolate chip or chocolate swirl brioche
200g unsalted butter, softened, plus extra for greasing
1 jar (about 340g) three-fruit marmalade
150ml milk
450ml double cream
4 eggs
4 tablespoons vanilla caster sugar

1 Butter an ovenproof dish.
2 Thinly slice the brioche and butter both sides. Spread half of the brioche slices with a layer of the marmalade, then make into sandwiches and cut each one in half to form triangles. Place the sandwiches at an angle in the buttered dish.
3 In a saucepan bring the milk and cream to the boil, then remove from the heat.
4 In a bowl whisk together the eggs and sugar until light and smooth. Gradually add the hot milk mixture to the egg mixture, whisking all the time.
5 Return the mixture to the saucepan and place over a low heat. Stir with a wooden spoon until the mixture thickens and just coats the back of the spoon – do not allow to boil or the eggs will scramble. When the mixture has thickened, pour evenly over the brioche triangles and leave to soak for 15 minutes. Preheat the oven to 150°C/gas mark 2.
6 Bake for 40–50 minutes. Serve warm.

Orange butter shortbread

A luxurious biscuit with citrus notes.

MAKES 20-25 BISCUITS

Equipment
Mixing bowl
Wooden spoon
Clingfilm
Large non-stick baking sheet
Sharp knife
Wire rack

225g soft unsalted butter
110g vanilla caster sugar, plus a little extra for sprinkling
225g plain flour, plus a little extra for rolling
110g cornflour
Finely grated zest of 1 large orange or 3 mandarins

1 In a bowl cream together the butter and sugar until light and
   fluffy.
2 Add the flour, cornflour and the zest and mix well to
   combine. You may need to knead briefly by hand to combine,
   but do not overwork the dough.
3 Dust a length of clingfilm with a little flour and turn out the
   shortbread dough onto it. Shape into a ball and wrap tightly.
   Chill in the fridge for half an hour so that the dough firms up.
4 Preheat the oven to 180°C/gas mark 4. Butter and flour your
   baking sheet.
5 Remove the dough from the fridge, unwrap and turn onto a
   lightly floured work surface. Divide the dough in half and roll
   each half into a cylinder about 5cm in diameter.
6 Cut 1cm thick discs from each cylinder and place on the
   baking sheet, leaving 3cm between each disc to allow for
   spreading. Bake for 10 minutes until cooked but not
   coloured.
7 Remove from the oven and sprinkle each biscuit with a
   pinch of caster sugar. The biscuits will still be soft, so leave
   to cool for 5 minutes on the baking sheet before removing to
   a wire rack to finish cooling. Best served while still warm.

Chocolate truffles

A smooth chocolate treat.

MAKES 20-30 TRUFFLES

Equipment
Saucepan
Spatula
3–6 small bowls
Sieve
Baking sheet
Greaseproof paper
Melon baller or very small ice cream scoop
Mug of just-boiled water
Fork
Cocktail sticks

175ml double cream
25g caster sugar
275g dark chocolate, broken up
30g unsalted butter, diced

Optional flavourings
1 mild chilli, very finely chopped
2 teaspoons spirit such as rum, brandy or whisky

Optional coatings
Cocoa powder, sifted
Melted white chocolate
Grated mint chocolate
Desiccated coconut
Chopped nuts

1   In a saucepan, bring the cream to the boil. Remove from the heat, add the sugar and the broken chocolate and stir until melted. Leave to cool for 5 minutes, then add the diced butter and stir until melted.
2   If you are using both flavourings, divide the truffle mix into three bowls and add the chilli to one bowl and the alcohol to another. Mix well to incorporate.
3   Cover and chill in the fridge for 4 hours or overnight.
4   Choose up to three different coatings and place each in a small bowl.
5   Cover a baking sheet with greaseproof paper.
6   Warm the baller in a mug of hot water and start balling the truffle mix, placing each truffle on the greaseproof paper and cleaning the baller in the hot water every two or three truffles.
7   When you have balled all the mix, roll the truffles individually in one of your dry coatings then return to the greaseproof paper to set.

Index